# REAL **BBQ**

# REAL BBQ

## THE ULTIMATE STEP-BY-STEP SMOKER COOKBOOK

WILL BUDIAMAN

ROCKRIDGE
PRESS

COVER PHOTOGRAPHS © Offset/Johnny Autry, Stockfood/Carmen Troesser, and Stockfood/Gräfe & Unzer Verlag/Grossmann Schuerle; INTERIOR PHOTOGRAPHS © Stocksy/Jeff Wasserman, p.2; Stocksy/Borislav Zhuykov, p.5; Stocksy/Javier Pardina, p.6; Stocksy/Julien L. Balmer, p.8; Stocksy/Leandro Crespi, p.10; Stocksy/Christine Han, p.12; Stocksy/Igor Madjinca, p.24; Stocksy/Javier Pardina, p.34; Stockfood/Sarah Coghill, p.36; Stockfood/Keller & Keller Photography, p.52; Stockfood/Carmen Troesser, p.66; Stocksy/J.R. Photography, p.80; Stockfood/Lars Ranek, p.94; Stocksy/Ilya, p.104; Stockfood/Gräfe & Unzer Verlag /Grossmann.Schuerle, p.134; Stocksy/Ben Ryan, p.158.

ISBN: Print 978-1-62315-600-8 | eBook 978-1-62315-601-5

## SMOKING MEAT 101

Real barbecue, or the art of cooking meat slow and steady with smoke, is all about time and patience. But understanding the process of smoking meat doesn't have to take all day. Follow these 5 simple steps and get started smoking up your own amazing barbecue in no time:

- ♦ Pick your fuel  (turn to page 22)

- ♦ Know your equipment (turn to page 26)

- ♦ Select your protein (turn to page 29)

- ♦ Kick up the flavor with a marinade, sauce, brine or rub (turn to page 105)

- ♦ Fire up your smoker and get smokin'!

# CONTENTS

# INTRODUCTION

Barbecue is everywhere today: from airport terminals around the world to cosmopolitan cities where it was once thought impossible to find true, down-home Southern cooking (hey, don't laugh—even New York City's got real barbecue these days). But wherever you find yourself enjoying some tender, juicy meat, all roads lead back to the four points of the barbecue compass: Texas, the Carolinas, Memphis, and Kansas City.

With barbecue's increase in popularity, it's easy to overlook what defines *real* barbecue. After all, in everyday conversation, people use the term casually. "Come on over; we're having a Fourth of July barbecue!" Thing is, if you're throwing burgers, steaks, and hot dogs on a grill for a hot second, that's not true barbecue; that's grilling. Real barbecue takes time, patience, and planning. Real barbecue is about sending tough, fatty cuts of meat through a transformative

cooking process, an effort rewarded with tender morsels that melt in your mouth. Real barbecue is smoked, flavored with hardwoods like apple, hickory, and oak. And that's the way it should be. So if you're ready to move on from the grill to tackle real barbecue, this is the book for you.

Part 1 covers everything you need to get started, with an overview of regional barbecue styles, as well as necessary equipment and ingredients. In Part 2, you'll learn the ins and outs of smoking particular proteins, which are highlighted with recipes that gradually incorporate more techniques, building your skill set and confidence as you go.

So, this isn't just another cookbook that you follow by the numbers. Instead, by the time you finish, you'll graduate from barbecue novice to pitmaster, and you'll have a true understanding of the technique.

# SMOKING FUNDAMENTALS

# CHAPTER ONE

# THE BASICS

Smoking meat is an art, and this chapter is all about the craft of real Southern barbecue. Though many different regional barbecue styles exist, four produce some of the tastiest, most distinctive barbecue in the country—Texas, the Carolinas, Memphis, and Kansas City. You'll find out about their defining characteristics and what makes them stand out from all the rest. And we'll help you choose a smoker that best suits your needs.

A note on smoking: There are two kinds of smoking—cold and hot. In both processes, smoke is used to flavor the food, but in the case of hot smoking, or barbecue, the food is cooked and smoked at the same time. This book focuses on hot smoking, since that's what barbecue is all about.

# THE ART OF SMOKING MEAT

What is the key ingredient in making real Southern barbecue? If you guessed smoke, you're right. These days, smokers come in all shapes and sizes, and they run on all kinds of power sources—natural gas, propane, charcoal, and even electricity. But the one thing they all have in common? They have to burn wood in some way to create the smoke that both cooks and flavors the protein.

## HOW SMOKING WORKS

Barbecue originally involved digging a pit in the ground, building a wood fire, and letting the fire burn down to embers. Then the meat slow-cooked on a spit over the embers and got smoked in the process. The modern-day equivalent of such a setup is a steel log pit whose exclusive fuel source is wood. And even if your setup isn't quite as fancy, the formula remains the same: smoke combined with low, indirect heat and plenty of time.

Smokers kick things up a few notches. Putting the meat in an enclosed apparatus versus cooking it in an open pit does two things: It shortens cooking time by trapping the heat, and it imparts greater flavor by trapping and circulating the smoke. The way smokers work today is pretty simple. The meat and heat source are separated, and wood is used to create smoke. In the case of wood-burning pits, wood also functions as the fuel. But generally, wood is added directly to the fuel or exposed to heat indirectly, causing it to smolder. Adjustable vents (and chimneys, depending on the design) provide a way to regulate temperature and smoke density, and they allow smoke to circulate and exit.

The choice of protein is also important. In America's early days, butchers and ranchers would save the large cuts of meat that were considered "less than choice" for themselves since they were difficult to sell. These cuts typically have a great deal of connective tissue and are tough and chewy when cooked using conventional methods. But early America's enterprising entrepreneurs discovered that if the undesirable cuts cooked on low heat for a long period of time, the meat would eventually turn tender and moist. That lip-smacking consistency is created when the collagen turns into gelatin, creating a perfectly cooked beef brisket or pulled pork shoulder. While these cuts still define traditional barbecue today, there is also

## Barbecue: A Presidential Tradition

Lyndon B. Johnson was the first president to hold a barbecue at the White House. His meat of choice? Texas-style ribs. Others have followed in his footsteps since, including Jimmy Carter and Ronald Reagan.

room for an expanded view of what you can smoke. These days meat choice isn't just about transforming the humbler cuts of meat. It's all about getting that delicious smoky flavor. You can smoke anything, chicken and fish included.

Part of the pleasure of barbecuing is that there is plenty of room for creativity. The technique is all about developing layers of flavor, and the first layer begins with the type of wood used to smoke the protein. Just about any type of hardwood can be used. Apple, cherry, and pear are a few popular fruitwoods, but non-fruitwood is also wonderful—hickory, oak, and cedar are solid choices. Some pitmasters like to mix and match the two types, and experimenting with different protein and wood pairings is part of the fun. Additional layers of flavor can be created through the use of dry rubs, wet rubs or pastes, brines, marinades, and finishing sauces, depending on which style of barbecue you want to make. All this will be covered in greater detail later on.

## THE 10 MOST PRESTIGIOUS BBQ COMPETITIONS IN AMERICA

You've got to admire the folks who choose to put everything on the line and enter a barbecue competition: They've got gumption, hauling their gear and sometimes families thousands of miles just to have a chance at winning. Some competitors have lots of money and the best equipment; others don't. But barbecue isn't just about throwing money around; sometimes the underdog wins. And that's the best part. Here are the ten greatest barbecue competitions in the country and the winning prizes.

◊ **Sam's Club National BBQ Tour.** Title of BBQ's National Champion and $500,000 in cash

◊ **American Royal World Series of Barbecue.** Winner takes home a $300,000 prize package

◊ **International Bar-B-Q Festival.** Governor's Cup awarded to best overall team

◊ **Memphis in May World Championship Barbecue Cooking Contest.** More than $110,000 worth of prizes

◊ **North Carolina State Barbecue Championship.** Winning team gets the Governor's Trophy

◊ **Safeway National Capital Barbecue Battle.** The title of America's BBQ Grand Champion and more than $40,000 in cash and prizes

◊ **Atlanta Bar-B-Q Festival.** More than $16,500 worth of prizes

◊ **Jack Daniel's World Championship Invitational Barbecue.** Title of Grand Champion and $10,000 in cash

◊ **World's Championship Bar-B-Que Contest.** Title of Overall Grand Champion

◊ **Hogs for the Cause.** Title of Ben Serrat Jr. "High on the Hog" Grand Champion

So, what are you waiting for? The big blue sky is calling, the breeze is just right, and there's a six-pack of beer sitting in the fridge with your name on it. It's time to go outside and make some barbecue.

# THE BEST BBQ IN AMERICA

Barbecue, like many great cuisines, had its beginnings in several different places at about the same time. That's why today you see many regional variations, each with its own nuances. And folks are fiercely proud of their style of barbecue; they'll swear that theirs is the only way to do barbecue. Still, if you were to take a road trip into the heart of barbecue country, there are four regions you wouldn't want to miss. The distinctive styles of these regions have been popularized into barbecue as we know it today.

## TEXAS

Though beef is the prevalent protein smoked in Texas, you'll find hog and even chicken in certain parts of the state.

Texas has several regional styles: Central Texas is known for smoked sausages, oak- or pecan-smoked brisket, and dry-rubbed ribs (both beef and pork), and they're not afraid to use mesquite, either, which can come off a bit strong. South Texas is *barbacoa* territory—which involves slow-cooking the head of a steer in a pit on the ground—while East Texas often relies on hickory and rebels against the rest of the republic by using sauce. And up in the Hill Country, they're known for something called "cowboy style." (Let your imagination run wild with that one.)

Texans usually like the flavor of the meat to come through, so it's very rare that sauce will make an appearance; if it does, it's usually served on the side, and it tends to be a smoky, tomato-based concoction flavored with dried ancho and guajillo chiles, a nod to the Mexican influence on the region's cooking. Instead, many Texan cooks rely on dry rubs to create a spiced crust around smoked meat, a trademark of the state's barbecue.

## MEMPHIS

In Memphis, folks are partial to pork ribs, both baby back and spare ribs. Like Texans, they prefer to stay away from sauce and stick to dry rubs to flavor their meat. However, you will find

### What's in a Name, Anyway?

Kansas City is what puts the "KC" in KC Masterpiece, which remains one of the most popular brands of barbecue sauce today. It was created by Rich Davis, a child psychiatrist turned restaurateur.

"wet" ribs as well as pulled pork. There, pulled pork is often topped with slaw and served in sandwiches. If there is sauce, it's a fairly mild one made with tomatoes.

## THE CAROLINAS

In the Carolinas, pork is the barbecue meat of choice. They sing the praises of pulled pork shoulder, and when it's time to celebrate a birthday, a wedding, or even the Fourth of July, they don't mess around—they bust out a whole hog and cook it low and slow.

The Carolinas have three main styles: Eastern North Carolina style is all about the whole hog. Barbecue from the entire pig is chopped up and mixed up with cracklin' (crunchy skin). In contrast, western North Carolina, or Lexington-style, barbecue focuses on pork shoulder. This geographical divide continues down to South Carolina.

When it comes to sauce, regional variations abound. In eastern North Carolina, folks swear by a simple, spicy concoction based on vinegar, while in western North Carolina, they prefer a mild, tomato-based sauce. And down in South Carolina, a hot and tangy mustard-based sauce is popular.

## KANSAS CITY

Kansas City can be described as the melting pot of barbecue—influences from the other three regions combine to create a unique style. Both beef and pork are equally loved, and pitmasters begin with a dry rub to coat their barbecue but might also finish it with a mild, tomato-based sauce. In fact, most of the prepared barbecue sauces that line supermarket shelves today are Kansas City style.

## GRILLING VS. SMOKING: WHAT'S THE DIFFERENCE?

When most people say they're having a barbecue, they're actually talking about grilling. True barbecue, however, involves smoking and is best done using a smoker, which separates the heat source from the food.

When you grill food, it's placed directly over a heat source and cooked at temperatures 300°F or higher for a brief period. When you barbecue, you hot smoke food, usually between temperatures of 200°F and 250°F. Most importantly, the food is placed away from the heat source, ideally in a separate compartment.

Grilling is great for tender, well-marbled cuts of meat like rib steaks, hamburger patties, thin cuts of meat, and small cuts of fish. Smoking works best on cuts of pork and beef that require extended cooking time to break down connective tissue, like beef brisket, pork butt, and spare ribs. It can also be used on seafood and poultry, mainly as a flavoring agent.

# TYPES OF SMOKERS

When it comes to buying a smoker, consumers really are spoiled for choice these days. There has been a slew of innovation in the past few decades, and budding barbecue enthusiasts can now expect great results from consumer-grade equipment.

While the type of smoker you choose—charcoal, electric, or wood—depends on your needs and preferences, there are a few things to consider no matter what type you decide to buy.

- **Size isn't everything, but it's definitely important.** Think about how many people you're planning on cooking for on a regular basis. If you're tackling big jobs like a whole pork shoulder or several racks of ribs at a time, it's important to make sure you've got enough real estate to play with. This is especially true if you're planning on using the indirect method on a conventional charcoal or gas grill (more on this below).

- **If it looks cheap, it *is* cheap.** If you want your smoker to last longer than the disposable aluminum pans you'll be using at your next barbecue, it's important to take construction into account. You want something sturdy that will stand the test of time. Stainless steel is often the material of choice, but bear in mind that it comes in different grades and thicknesses; some manufacturers cut costs by constructing the lid and grates out of stainless steel but opting for a cheaper material for the frame. Welding is also an indicator of quality: Is the join smooth and continuous, or is it spotty, just enough to hold the joints together?

- **Yeah, it's hot, but is it too hot?** This may seem pretty obvious, but if the smoker doesn't have a built-in thermometer to tell you how hot the cooking compartment is, it's not worth buying. Since smoking relies on maintaining a constant temperature over a long period of time, having an accurate thermometer is key. Low-end models tend to skimp on this feature. Instead, they come equipped with gauges that display temperature zones instead of numerical readouts, which is not terribly helpful.

## CHARCOAL SMOKERS

Charcoal smokers come in various designs, but they all have a firebox (the chamber where the charcoal and wood go) that is separate from the cooking compartment (where the protein goes). Following are some of the more popular choices.

Offset models have a firebox off to the side of the cooking compartment. The cooking compartment looks like an oil drum cut in half to create a hinged opening. The smoke enters the cooking compartment through an opening from the firebox. You adjust the temperature by opening and closing vents; opening a vent allows greater airflow and stokes the fire, while closing it cools things down. A chimney at one end of the cooking compartment allows smoke to escape and promotes circulation.

Vertical water smokers circulate moisture in addition to smoke, making them ideal for barbecuing lean meats, poultry, and fish. The moisture can come from water, fruit juices, broth, beer, or anything else you'd like to flavor your protein with. Vertical smokers tend to have

## HORIZONTAL OFFSET SMOKER

Chimney

Thermometer

Smoking chamber

Fire Box

Door vents

Charcoal grate

## VERTICAL WATER SMOKER

Thermometer

Lid

Access door

Top grate

Smoking chamber

Bottom grate

Water pan

Charcoal pan

some difficulty with fattier cuts of meat like beef brisket and pork shoulder, though, since the moisture hinders the rendering of the fat, resulting in 'cue that's still got a bit too much jiggle attached to the muscle. But they do start cheap—about $50 for a small charcoal burner—and if charcoal's not your thing, you can find models that run on electricity and gas. They're all similarly designed: bullet-shaped, with a bubble-shaped lid revealing an interior with one or two grates, and below it, a drip pan for holding the moistening liquid. Underneath that is where the charcoal and wood goes.

## ELECTRIC SMOKERS

Electric smokers are a bit like the slow cooker of the barbecue world. They're simple and convenient to use, look more like regular kitchen appliances, and provide even, consistent heat. All you need to do is replenish the wood occasionally to keep the smoke going, and some models even eliminate that step. Of course, some people complain that with all of the convenience, it doesn't feel like you're really barbecuing. It all seems too civilized—a bit like having HAL 9000 cook your brisket.

Electric vertical water smokers are more expensive than their charcoal counterparts but provide convenience by eliminating the need to add charcoal regularly.

Pellet smokers burn even-size pellets of wood that come in different flavors and have a mechanical feeder that eliminates the need to add wood. There are also models that use briquettes in a similar fashion.

## WOOD SMOKERS

Wood smokers tend to be suited for big jobs like smoking whole hogs, so they often have the largest footprint. They provide the most intense smoke flavor, and professional-grade smokers can accept whole logs of wood as a fuel source. They have the same design as charcoal offset smokers, just larger.

The downside tends to be price. Although you can now find consumer models of steel log pits that burn wood chunks, even entry-level models will set you back at least a few hundred dollars. Still, if that's the way you want to go, you can find them at home improvement stores and most retailers that sell regular grills.

## SMOKING ON THE GRILL

If you're interested in smoking meat but not quite ready to invest in any new equipment, it's still possible to enjoy real barbecue. Using your existing charcoal or gas grill, you can create an

### The World's Largest BBQ Pit

Yes, it's in Texas (of course). The world's largest barbecue pit weighs 80,000 pounds, is 75 feet long, has 2 dozen doors, and can barbecue 8,000 pounds of meat at once. The price tag? A cool $350,000.

indirect heat source that allows you to smoke your protein.

On a charcoal grill, mound all of the charcoal off to one side in a single layer, light it, and let it burn down to embers. (Alternatively, you can mound the charcoal around the perimeter.) If you're using a gas grill, it has to have at least two burners. Light one side and leave the other off. On a three-burner grill, light the burners on the outer edges. In any of these setups, place the protein over the unheated section.

To create the wood smoke, first soak hardwood chips in water for at least half an hour, then wrap them in foil. Poke several holes in the foil for smoke to vent, and place the packet over the heat source on the grill. Close the lid to begin smoking.

There are two disadvantages to this method. First, since you cannot place the protein directly over the fuel source, there's always going to be a portion of the cooking area you won't be able to use. Second, some people believe that for thicker, larger cuts of meat (those requiring more than a couple of hours of smoking), the smoke flavor doesn't penetrate very well to the center.

## SMOKER MAINTENANCE

These 10 tips will help keep your smoker in tip-top shape:

◊ **Clean while hot.** Always clean the grates right after cooking. If you let the surface cool, anything that's stuck to the grates will become much harder to remove.

◊ **Oil it up.** Use an oil-soaked rag and a pair of tongs to oil up the grates after you're done cleaning, so it's ready to go for the next barbecue.

◊ **Season regularly.** Apply food-grade mineral oil to the grates and let the smoker run for at least a couple hours at normal temperatures to protect against rust.

◊ **Scrape it down.** Over time, the layer of seasoning can flake away. Be sure to scrape away any flakes and reseason; you don't want this stuff to end up in your food.

◊ **Prevent flare-ups.** A thorough scrub of the entire interior once a year is a great idea. This will get rid of all the accumulated debris that could lead to spontaneous flare-ups. Use an oven-safe cleaner and scrub brush. For tougher jobs, a paint scraper can be used.

◊ **Buy a cover.** A snug-fitting cover protects your smoker from the elements when not in use.

◊ **Don't forget the chimney.** If your cooker has one, make sure to clean it out regularly; over time, buildup can reduce the effectiveness of your smoker.

◊ **Get rid of ash.** Allowing ash to collect promotes rusting, since it attracts ambient moisture.

◊ **Inspect for rust.** Look for signs of rusting on a regular basis. If you find rust, scrape it away and repaint or reseason as needed.

# FUEL

To create the heat needed to cook your barbecue, your smoker will run on charcoal, gas, or wood. Each of these heat sources has its benefits and challenges.

## CHARCOAL

Charcoal is inexpensive and gives protein some of the smoky flavor sought after in barbecue, but for best results you'll want to combine it with soaked wood chips, placed directly on top of the embers after the fire burns out. Charcoal burns hot, so it can be tough for beginners to control. This can make it complicated to determine cooking times. Cleanup can also be messy, and you'll need to stick around to add more charcoal to the cooker regularly; figure on having to add charcoal every hour or so. How much you need to add every hour depends on the weather, your smoker's size and insulation, and whether you are using lump charcoal or briquettes. In addition, you'll want to have the next batch of charcoal you're adding lit in advance—a process which takes 20 to 30 minutes—so the temperature doesn't drop too much when you add it. However, there are ways of dealing with these issues. An ash catcher makes cleanup easier, and a good charcoal smoker should have adjustable vents on the top and bottom to regulate the heat.

Charcoal is available in two varieties: briquette and lump. Charcoal briquettes are made from compressed hardwood that is bound together using chemical additives, some of which are known carcinogens. But briquettes are friendlier for novices. They burn more uniformly owing to their shape, making it easier to maintain a steady temperature. Do not buy "self-starting" briquettes for barbecuing, since they are soaked in petroleum-based lighter fluid. Lump charcoal does not contain additives, but it burns hotter and can be difficult to transport since it is fragile.

## GAS

Natural gas and propane smokers are great choices for beginners. Unlike charcoal, there's no messy cleanup, and the fuel is relatively cheap. Gas smokers start quickly, and the temperature is easier to control than with charcoal smokers. However, gas smokers are a bit pricier, and the fuel source doesn't add any smoky flavor on its own—which is not necessarily a disadvantage, since some form of wood is always needed to generate smoke.

## WOOD

No matter what kind of smoker you have, you'll always need to have wood chips on hand to create the smoke that flavors the protein. However, you can also use wood as the fuel source. The benefit is obvious: You get the most smoke flavor this way. But for delicate proteins like poultry and lean fish, this method can be overpowering. Furthermore, picking up a bag of wood chips to flavor meat is easy; finding enough wood chunks or logs to burn as a fuel source can be a challenge, unless you happen to have a forest in your backyard. Still, some manufacturers have found a way around this problem by creating electrically powered smokers that burn uniform wood pellets or briquettes (see "Electric Smokers" for more details).

# FROM THE PITMASTER

**HARRISON SAPP**
**PROPRIETOR AND PITMASTER, SOUTHERN SOUL BARBEQUE**
www.southernsoulbbq.com

*What tips and tricks can you offer on maximizing the flavor of your barbecue?*

At Southern Soul, we source the best ingredients and treat them with the utmost respect on the way to creating the most flavorful barbecue possible. We follow a few simple tips that ought to be helpful to anyone:

**Lighter fluid: Don't buy it.** You are cooking something that will take hours. Why risk messing it all up before you even get started? When it comes to barbecue, the worst taste of all is lighter fluid.

**Rub: Let it sink in.** Letting the rub sit on the protein for a few minutes on small cuts or overnight for large cuts will allow the spices to flavor the inside, not just the outside. If you're letting it sit overnight, do it in the refrigerator, of course.

**Sauce at the end.** If you're using sauce, don't put it on your protein until it is finished. Any sugar in the sauce will just burn.

**Use raw sugars for rubs.** It won't burn as easily, and it makes a great bark (crust). I can always tell when someone uses processed sugar for their rubs. It tastes and smells burnt to me.

**Write down everything you do.** That way, if you like or dislike your 'cue you can replicate or fix it. Barbecue diaries are good to have.

*Harrison Sapp is the proprietor and pitmaster at Southern Soul Barbeque in St. Simons Island, Georgia. His award-winning barbeque has earned distinction among locals and has been featured on Food Network's* Diners, Drive-ins, and Dives *and in* Southern Living *and* The Huffington Post.

# CHAPTER TWO

# GETTING STARTED

Great! You've got your smoker. Now, what else do you need to get started? This chapter covers all the paraphernalia necessary to begin cookin' some amazing 'cue. It is tough not to feel a bit like a kid in a candy store the first time you walk into a barbecue supply shop or the outdoor cooking section of the hardware store, but a quick read through the Tools and Equipment section in this chapter will help you separate wants from needs.

You'll also learn how to select the best cuts of meat for your barbecue, how to get wood, how to stock your pantry well enough to whip up a dry rub or sauce at a moment's notice, and a few basic tips and techniques that will help anyone make great barbecue.

# TOOLS AND EQUIPMENT

Some tools and equipment, the essentials, should be on everyone's shopping list. There are also fun toys for the barbecue master that aren't absolutely necessary for basic barbecue but would be great to have.

## THE ESSENTIALS

* **Thermometers.** Look for an instant-read thermometer that can withstand the heat of the smoker so you can insert it into the protein and leave it there. This way, you won't have to keep poking at the meat to take temperature readings, letting juices leak out. You'll also want to get an oven thermometer that you can place on the smoker grate to get a surface reading where the meat is cooking. Although this may seem unnecessary if your smoker has a built-in thermometer, a second reading will ensure that your meat cooks at the correct

* **Tongs.** This versatile kitchen tool is great for everything from picking up proteins and moving them around to handling hot chunks of wood and charcoal. Choose sturdy, long-handled tongs that can close all the way. How long should the arms be? Choose a size you're comfortable working with; just make sure that they're long enough to isolate your hands from the heat of the grill. Avoid self-locking tongs; they may seem neat, but they'll quickly become an annoyance.

* **Spatula.** Choose a sturdy one with an insulated handle. A spatula is great for transferring smaller, delicate pieces of protein like fish fillets, and it can also be used together with tongs to move larger proteins.

* **Grill brush.** You need one to clean the grates. Either purchase cheap ones frequently or buy pricier ones in the hope that they'll last longer. Either way, check often to make sure bristles haven't fallen out. They're not fun to eat.

* **Timer.** Get one so you don't lose track of time and overcook your protein. Larger, fattier cuts tend to be more forgiving, but leaner, smaller cuts of fish and poultry require closer watch.

* **Cutting boards.** Buy two: a nonporous one for raw meat that can be sanitized, and another one for slicing cooked meats.

* **Sharp knife.** Any good chef's knife in a comfortable size from a reputable brand like Henckels, Global, or Wüsthof will do.

* **Aluminum foil.** This kitchen staple is handy for keeping meat warm after cooking. It's also a must-have if you're using the indirect method with a regular grill (see page 20, "Smoking on the Grill"), unless you have a smoker box.

* **Disposable aluminum pans.** These make it easy to store and transport large cuts of protein after cooking. They can also double as drip pans that will circulate moisture and capture fat as it drips through the grates, if your smoker doesn't have one or if you're using a regular grill.

- **Small kitchen towel.** A towel makes oiling up the grill a snap. Roll it up and lightly coat it with vegetable oil. Grab with a pair of tongs and swab the grates with it.

- **Large sealable plastic bags.** Unless you're doing a whole pork shoulder, these should serve most of your initial marinating needs.

- **Chimney starter.** If you have a charcoal smoker, forget lighter fluid. Using this simple tool is the safest way to start a charcoal fire.

- **Barbecue lighter.** These have longer necks, so they're easier to use than regular lighters, especially when you're starting a charcoal fire.

- **Fire extinguisher.** You may need one to put out a fire.

## FOR THE MASTER

- **Spice grinder.** Toasting spices whole and grinding them yourself adds depth and complexity to sauces and rubs.

- **Basting brush.** Use it to apply sauces to proteins toward the end of the cooking time, giving them a finishing glaze. This step isn't always necessary, but it can be a nice touch.

- **Heat-resistant gloves.** You can find gloves that cover your entire arms. They're probably overkill if you're just starting out, but one day when you find yourself working with large cuts of protein on a regular basis, it's often easier to just pick them up with your hands than to use tongs and a spatula together.

- **Bear paws.** These look like giant plastic combs with widely spaced tines and are specifically designed for shredding meat. If you love making pulled pork or chicken, this is the tool for you. Sure, you could just use a couple of forks, but these are way more fun.

- **Smoker box.** If you use the indirect method on a conventional grill, this perforated metal box that holds wood chips and can be placed directly on the grates is a handy alternative to wrapping chips in foil every time.

- **Large nonreactive containers.** Glass or food-grade plastic containers are great for marinating large cuts of meat like whole pork shoulder or a whole turkey. Avoid aluminum ones because the metal reacts with marinades containing acid (which is just about all of them).

- **Kitchen syringe.** If you're starting to work regularly with large cuts of protein, you may want to consider injecting your marinades, which helps them penetrate much better than simply bathing your proteins.

- **Fine-meshed strainer.** If you're going to inject marinades, you'll want to strain out any bits and pieces of herbs or spices that could clog the syringe.

- **Shovel.** If you have a really, really big wood-burning steel pit, a shovel will make loading wood chunks into the firebox much easier. At this point, it's probably safe to say you're beyond using tongs.

# FROM THE PITMASTER

**JOHN GRIGSBY**
**UNCLE BUTCH BBQ**
www.unclebutch.com

***What's the smoking tool (besides your smoker) you couldn't do without?***

When we compete, the tool we rely on the most is the thermometer. We place one in our brisket and one in our pork butt, so we stop them cooking at just the correct temperature. Competition smoking isn't about having the tenderest meat; it is about having meat that has the right pull. We purchased a Guru with our new smokers. The Guru gives the temperature inside the smoker and inside the meat. We also have a Maverick that we have used in the past. I am not hung up on all the gadgets that come with some of the other ones; I just want to know the temperature of the meat. We visually monitor the temperature and know about when the briskets and pork butts should be ready based upon our cooking temperature.

*John Grigsby and his father have been competing together at the Kansas City barbecue competitions for five years. Their team, Uncle Butch BBQ, has four smokers that they rotate in and out of use for different types of barbecue. He helped his father custom-build their very first smoker, made from a 250-gallon barrel, for their first competition. It was truly a labor of love. Ever since then, Grigsby has been hooked, and he has welcomed the opportunity to do something competitive with his father.*

*The team's specialty is pulled pork barbecue sandwiches with homemade mild barbecue sauce, and they cater locally when not competing. Grigsby hails from Knoxville, Tennessee.*

# SELECTING YOUR PROTEIN

As with any other type of cooking, what you get out of barbecuing is only as good as the ingredients you put into it. This makes sense with a cooking method that is all about showcasing the natural flavor of the meat.

Whenever possible, select meat from sustainable, responsibly raised sources for maximum flavor; happy animals make for better-tasting meat.

## PORK

When it comes to pork, bigger is better. Why? Because larger cuts of pork generally contain more collagen, and more collagen means a better eating experience, translating to the lip-smacking consistency you want when eating good barbecued pork.

Of course, it's important to keep an eye on quality, too. When shopping for pork, look for evenly distributed, thin lines of fat throughout the muscle. Avoid any meat that has large chunks of fat in the center. Most importantly, don't buy frozen meat; freezing destroys the texture of the meat.

As far as cuts go, any part of the animal that sees a whole lot of exercise, like the shoulder, ham, and trotters, are all good bets because they'll contain plenty of collagen.

## BEEF

Figuring out which cuts of beef to buy for barbecue isn't terribly different from doing the same with pork. Aim for parts of the animal that move a lot; cuts like brisket and shank work particularly well.

Unlike pork, beef comes in different grades. These are determined by the USDA and are a measure of marbling, or the quantity and quality of fat that is spread throughout the muscle. Fat content is important to consider because fat is an excellent carrier of aromatic compounds and flavors.

There are three grades: Prime, Choice, and Select. For barbecuing, Prime is definitely overkill. While it's important to have some marbling, too much marbling is basically money down the drain, since the long cooking process will cause excess fat to drip out of the meat. If you're buying Prime, stick to grilling; don't smoke it. Select tends to have fat that is low in quality; often, instead of thin lines of fat, you'll see chunks. Choice is the happy medium.

## CHICKEN

Chicken doesn't have a whole lot of fat or collagen, so the criteria for picking chicken are entirely different.

Because the bird has mild flavor, sticking to whole chickens is preferable when barbecuing. But if you want to start small, opt for bone-in, skin-on cuts to maximize flavor. Air-chilled chicken is also a smart buy; most chicken gets dunked in a water bath during processing, adding water weight (that you pay for) and diluting flavor. Those who swear by air-chilled chicken say it's worth the slight premium and tastes more "chicken-y," like the stuff their grandparents used to get.

# SOURCING WOOD

Wood is an indispensable ingredient for flavoring your barbecued meats, poultry, and fish, regardless of the type of fuel that powers your smoker. It may even be your flavoring agent *and* fuel source. So depending on your needs, sourcing wood can be a bit tricky. Here are a few pointers to help you get started.

- **Try the hardware store.** This should be the first stop for most people. If you're looking for wood chips or chunks, you will probably find them here. If you need whole logs, you may need to look elsewhere.

- **Go to a specialty retailer.** Stores that specialize in selling grills and smokers will often sell wood chips or chunks. If you have an electric smoker that uses pellets or briquettes, this is also a logical place to look.

- **Find a firewood dealer.** There are plenty of online directories, such as Log Splitter (logsplitter.com), that list firewood dealers by state. If you need whole logs, this is a good option. Some dealers are willing to deliver, but this can get pricey.

- **When all else fails, ask around.** Unless you live in the middle of a desert, you'll probably find someone who has either some wood to spare or a tree that needs trimming. Even if you don't exactly have a forest in your backyard, chances are a neighbor has a fruit tree that's becoming a bit unruly, or someone at the local farmers' market might be willing to bring you some wood the next time you see them. You can also try posting classifieds, either in print or online on a service like Craigslist. Just make sure that the person on the other end seems reputable and is selling you wood that's safe to use.

- **Above all, choose the right type of wood.** It may seem convenient, but sourcing wood scraps from a construction site or using plywood is definitely unsafe. Those types of woods usually have been treated with chemicals that you don't want ending up in your food. There are also certain types of trees you should steer clear of—anything soft and resinous will impart a bitter flavor and make you sick. Avoid species like elm, eucalyptus, fir, pine, redwood, spruce, and sycamore. In general, stick to hardwoods from fruit or nut trees and certain other species like hickory and oak (see the sidebar "Flavors of Wood" for a list of suggested types).

# FLAVORS OF WOOD

Part of the fun when it comes to barbecue is figuring out how different types of wood interact with different proteins. Of course, the choices of wood available to you will depend on where you live, but chances are you'll be able to play around a little bit. One interesting thing you may want to try is pairing fruitwoods in different proportions with non-fruitwoods.

Here are descriptions of some of the most common types of hardwood suitable for barbecue, along with suggested pairings—emphasis on "suggested," since this is more subjective than it is an exact science.

## FRUITWOODS

◊ **Apple.** Delicate. The flavor and aroma of apple-wood and pork were made for each other.

◊ **Apricot.** Assertive, sweet. Ideal with poultry like chicken and duck.

◊ **Cherry.** Balanced sweetness. Can be used with all manner of meats, poultry, and seafood.

◊ **Olive.** Great if you're looking for something different. Flavor depends on tree varietal. Can be rich, nutty, fruity, or even a bit spicy. Use with lean cuts that can act as a "canvas," such as chicken breast or pork tenderloin.

◊ **Orange.** Sweet, citrusy. Great for chicken, duck, or seafood.

◊ **Peach.** Assertive, sweet. Great with pork.

◊ **Plum.** Surprisingly delicate sweetness. Try it with duck if you want the flavor of the meat to dominate; also good with turkey.

## NUTWOODS

◊ **Almond.** Mellow sweetness that goes well with just about anything.

◊ **Pecan.** Similar to almond. Some say that it's hickory's mellower brother.

◊ **Walnut.** Bold flavor. Has an astringency that can overpower. Use sparingly together with other types of wood.

## OTHER HARDWOODS

◊ **Alder.** Similar to cedar.

◊ **Cedar.** Matches perfectly with salmon. Also good with chicken.

◊ **Hickory.** Bold, sharp flavors make it strong enough to stand up to beef. Great with lamb as well.

◊ **Maple.** Possesses a unique and pleasant sweetness that goes particularly well with— you guessed it—pork. Great with chicken, too.

◊ **Oak.** Falls in the same category as hickory. Use for beef and lamb.

# THE SMOKER PANTRY

Your pantry is where marinades, brines, dry rubs, pastes, and sauces come from. And those things can elevate good barbecue to great barbecue—by creating layers of flavor before, during, and after the cooking process. So keeping the pantry well stocked is an important step in staying prepared. Here are some suggested herbs, spices, condiments, and other essentials to keep on hand. This list is by no means exhaustive, but it is a good place to start.

## HERBS AND SPICES

Allspice, whole

Cayenne pepper

Chili powder, chipotle

Chili powder, guajillo

Chili powder, regular

Cinnamon, ground

Cloves, whole

Coriander, ground

Cumin, whole

Mustard, yellow, ground

Nutmeg, whole

Old Bay Seasoning

Oregano, dried

Oregano, Mexican, dried

Paprika, hot

Paprika, smoked

Paprika, sweet

Peppercorns, black

Peppercorns, white

Red pepper flakes

Salt, Kosher

Sesame seeds, white

## OTHER PANTRY ESSENTIALS

Broth, beef

Broth, chicken

Chiles, red, dried

Coffee, instant

Garlic, fresh

Honey

Jalapeños, fresh

Juice, apple

Juice, orange

Juice, pineapple

Ketchup

Lemons

Limes

Mayonnaise

Molasses, blackstrap, unfiltered

Mustard, yellow

Oil, vegetable

Olive oil, extra-virgin

Onions, fresh

Parsley, Italian, fresh

Soy sauce

Sugar, dark brown

Sugar, turbinado

Sugar, white, granulated

Thyme, fresh

Tomato paste, canned

Tomato purée, canned

Vinegar, apple cider

Vinegar, white, distilled

Worcestershire sauce

# A FEW FINAL TIPS

Now that you have everything you need to get started, these ten tips are the perfect send-off; keep these in mind and you will be a master of the art and craft of barbecue in no time.

◊ **Make sure you have enough fuel.**
Nothing's worse than running out of wood, charcoal, or gas in the middle of a barbecue.

**Take off the chill.** Allow meat to come to room temperature before placing it in the smoker. This is especially important for large cuts of meat to promote even cooking.

**Leave it alone.** Once the meat goes into the cooking compartment, don't look at it. Every time you open the lid, you lose heat and add an average of 15 minutes to the cooking time. Barbecue already takes long enough; why add to the suspense?

**Easy with the sauce now.** Some regional styles of barbecue don't even call for sauce and consider it sacrilege—hello, Texas!—but if you'd like some sauce on your ribs, use at the end. Most sauces contain a fair amount of sugar that will burn if you put it on at the beginning. Open the lid in the last 15 to 30 minutes of cooking, slather it on as quickly as you can, and shut the lid.

**Hey, careful where you stick that thing.** There's a right way to insert a thermometer into a piece of meat. Find the thickest part of the cut and insert the probe as far as it will go without touching the bone, if there is one.

**Sometimes too much information is a bad thing.** If you've got a fancy thermometer with a remote probe that allows you to monitor the temperature of the meat without opening the lid, good for you. But you may notice the temperature of the meat stops climbing for a while. Don't worry; this is normal. When you're cooking with indirect heat, temperatures rarely climb in a steady thrust to the top. There are various theories as to why it happens, but the important thing is: Relax, it's fine.

**Give it a rest.** Whatever you've cooked has just spent several hours in a hot box. Let it rest before slicing to allow the juices to redistribute.

**Drip, drip, drip.** If your smoker doesn't come with a water pan, position a disposable aluminum pan underneath the grate where the meat cooks. You can use this pan to add liquids that will moisten and flavor the meat, and it will also keep fat from hitting the metal below and generating carcinogens.

**Keep that water pan filled.** If you're using a vertical water smoker, it's very important to periodically check on the water pan. If it runs dry, the temperature in the cooking compartment can spike suddenly.

**Keep the charcoal and wood coming.** The same goes for fuel if you're using wood, charcoal, or a combination of both. If you don't replenish about once an hour, the temperature could drop quickly.

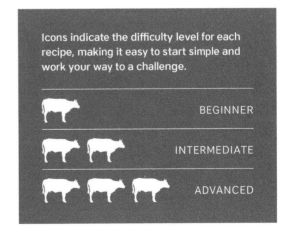

Icons indicate the difficulty level for each recipe, making it easy to start simple and work your way to a challenge.

BEGINNER

INTERMEDIATE

ADVANCED

**PART TWO**

# LET'S SMOKE SOME MEAT

# CHAPTER THREE

# POULTRY

Although poultry may not register as strongly as pork or beef on the radar of traditional barbecue fanatics, it certainly deserves a place at the table. In this chapter, you'll learn how to turn out flavorful, juicy chicken and turkey every time.

# TECHNIQUES

In the barbecuing world, poultry is in an entirely different class than beef or pork. If you were to smoke poultry the same way you would pork or beef, you'd probably end up with some pretty tough, flavorless, dry birds. Here's why: Chickens and their relatives are lean animals that don't have a lot of connective tissue, which means that even with a low and slow smoke, they should not spend too much time cooking (especially when separated into different cuts). There also isn't as much leeway when it comes to cooking times: large, fatty cuts of pork and beef can see up to an hour of cooking time over the range recommended in a recipe with little ill effect, whereas poultry needs to be monitored closely.

There are a few ways you can enhance flavors before putting the bird in the smoker. Brining—especially the breasts, which tend to dry out during cooking—is an excellent way to season poultry. Chapter 8, "Sauces, Rubs, Brines, and Marinades," covers how brining works in greater detail.

Marinades are also good for achieving tasty results, but they tend to work better on individual cuts of poultry for shorter periods of time because they contain acidic ingredients that can cause the flesh to turn rubbery if bathed for too long.

Rubs are also an effective technique for heightening flavor.

Poultry should be cooked to an internal temperature of 165°F. Use an instant-read thermometer inserted into the thickest part of the meat without touching the bone to keep a constant read on the internal temperature. Because your protein will continue to cook as it rests after you pull it out of the smoker, you can pull it out about 5 degrees early.

To make sure the flesh stays juicy, it's important to keep the skin on even though the low and slow cooking process will turn it rubbery. Once the bird is done smoking, you can crisp up the skin in a hot skillet with a bit of oil.

# SMOKED HOT WINGS

**SERVES 4 TO 6**

PREP TIME: 30 MINUTES

COOK TIME: 2 TO 2 ½ HOURS

RECOMMENDED WOOD: PECAN

2 pounds chicken wings
or drumettes

Vegetable oil, for brushing
the grates

2 tablespoons Hot 'n' Tangy
Dry Rub (page 123)

1 cup Buffalo Sauce (page 108)

Whether you're hosting a big Super Bowl bash or just having some friends over for a few beers on a lazy Sunday afternoon, these hot wings are sure to impress. After you've had smoked hot wings, the whole "baked vs. fried" debate no longer exists. Neither can match the flavor of smoked.

1. Soak 3 cups of wood chips in water for 15 to 30 minutes.

2. Wash the chicken and pat it dry. Let it come to room temperature.

3. Preheat the smoker to 225°F to 250°F, and add the wood chips, following the manufacturer's instructions.

4. If the grates haven't been oiled: Roll up a clean, lint-free kitchen towel and dip it into some vegetable oil. Using tongs, grab the towel and rub it across the grates.

5. Coat the chicken thoroughly in the dry rub, and place it on the grates in a single layer.

6. Close the cooking compartment and smoke for 2 to 2½ hours, or until an instant-read thermometer inserted into the flesh without touching the bone reads at least 160°F. Soak additional wood chips and replenish as needed; if you no longer see smoke exiting the chimneys or vents, add more wood.

7. Transfer to a large bowl and toss with the wing sauce. Serve immediately.

**TROUBLESHOOTING** To help the dry rub adhere, try rubbing the wings with a bit of vegetable oil first.

# SMOKED CHICKEN DRUMSTICKS

**SERVES 4 TO 6**

PREP TIME: 30 MINUTES

COOK TIME: 2 ½ TO 3 HOURS

RECOMMENDED WOOD: ORANGE

2 pounds chicken drumsticks

2 tablespoons "Good on Everything" Dry Rub (page 121)

2 tablespoons vegetable oil, plus more for brushing the grates

Because drumsticks are one of the more flavorful chicken parts to begin with, brining isn't necessary. A tasty dry rub is all you need. Shred leftover meat for dishes like Kicked-Up Chicken-Tortilla Soup (page 44).

**1.** Soak 4½ cups of wood chips in water for 15 to 30 minutes.

**2.** Wash the chicken and pat it dry. Let it come to room temperature.

**3.** Preheat the smoker to 225°F to 250°F and add the wood chips, following the manufacturer's instructions.

**4.** If the grates haven't been oiled: Roll up a clean, lint-free kitchen towel and dip it into some vegetable oil. Using tongs, grab the towel and rub it across the grates.

**5.** Coat the chicken thoroughly in the dry rub and place it on the grates in a single layer.

**6.** Close the cooking compartment and smoke for 2½ to 3 hours, or until an instant-read thermometer inserted into the flesh without touching the bone reads at least 160°F. Soak additional wood chips and replenish as needed; if you no longer see smoke exiting the chimneys or vents, add more wood.

**7.** In a large sauté pan, heat the 2 tablespoons of vegetable over high heat. When the oil is hot add the drumsticks, and brown all over for 3 to 5 minutes, or until the skin is crisp. Let the drumsticks rest for 5 minutes before serving.

**PAIR IT** Try serving this with "Sweet Home Alabama" Barbecue Sauce (page 118).

# SMOKY, SPICY CHICKEN THIGHS

**SERVES 4 TO 6**

PREP TIME: 30 MINUTES

COOK TIME: 2½ TO 3 HOURS

RECOMMENDED WOOD: PECAN

2 pounds bone-in, skin-on chicken thighs

2 tablespoons Texas Dry Rub (page 125)

2 tablespoons vegetable oil, plus more for brushing the grates

The bold flavors of guajillo, chipotle, and ancho chilies are a good match for chicken thighs. After a few hours of smoking, they turn unbelievably juicy and tender. A quick sear at the end caramelizes the sugars in the rub and crisps up the skin.

**1.** Soak 4½ cups of wood chips in water for 15 to 30 minutes.

**2.** Wash the chicken and pat it dry. Let it come to room temperature.

**3.** Preheat the smoker to 225°F to 250°F and add the wood chips, following the manufacturer's instructions.

**4.** If the grates haven't been oiled: Roll up a clean, lint-free kitchen towel and dip it into some vegetable oil. Using tongs, grab the towel and rub it across the grates.

**5.** Coat the chicken thoroughly in the dry rub and place it on the grates in a single layer.

**6.** Close the cooking compartment and smoke for 2½ to 3 hours, or until an instant-read thermometer inserted into the flesh without touching the bone reads at least 160°F. Soak additional wood chips and replenish as needed; if you no longer see smoke exiting the chimneys or vents, add more wood.

**7.** In a large sauté pan, heat the 2 tablespoons of vegetable oil over high heat. When the oil is hot, add the thighs and brown skin-side down for 1½ to 2 minutes, or until the skin is crisp. Rest for 5 minutes before serving.

**SMOKING TIP** Soaking wood chips keeps them from burning up right away when you add them to the firebox, especially on charcoal.

# BARBECUE CHICKEN SALAD WITH BUTTERMILK DRESSING

**SERVES 2**

PREP TIME: 5 MINUTES

COOK TIME: 4 MINUTES

2 strips bacon

8 cups mixed greens, such as frisée, radicchio, and endive

½ fennel bulb, cored and thinly sliced

3 tablespoons Buttermilk Dressing (page 109)

1 smoked chicken breast, sliced

2 tablespoons Kansas City–Style Barbecue Sauce (page 111; optional)

Looking for an interesting salad for lunch? Look no further. Tangy buttermilk dressing is the perfect backdrop for bitter greens and smoked chicken breasts.

**1.** In a sauté pan, cook the bacon over high heat for 1 ½ to 2 minutes, or until crisp on one side.

**2.** Reduce the heat to medium, flip the bacon, and cook the other side for 1 to 2 minutes.

**3.** Remove the bacon and set aside.

**4.** In a large bowl, toss the mixed greens and fennel with the buttermilk dressing, and crumble the bacon on top.

**5.** Divide between 2 plates and top with the chicken. Drizzle the chicken with the barbecue sauce (if using), and serve immediately.

**PAIR IT** For a more substantial meal, serve with a side of Grilled Corn on the Cob with Herb Butter (page 146).

# BARBECUE CHICKEN SLIDERS WITH SIMPLE SLAW

**SERVES 4**

PREP TIME: 5 MINUTES

4 slider rolls, split

1 smoked chicken breast, thinly sliced

1 cup Simple Cole Slaw (page 138)

¼ cup Kansas City–Style Barbecue Sauce (page 111)

These sliders are simple to make and unbelievably delicious. This recipe can easily be scaled up to feed a crowd. For the best sliders, look for brioche buns.

**1.** On the heel of each bun, place one-quarter of the sliced chicken and top with coleslaw.

**2.** Drizzle barbecue sauce over the coleslaw, and top with the crown of the bun.

**PAIR IT** To turn this into a complete meal, serve the sliders with some Classic Potato Salad (page 151).

# KICKED-UP CHICKEN-TORTILLA SOUP

**SERVES 8**

PREP TIME: 15 MINUTES

COOK TIME: 40 MINUTES

1 tablespoon cumin seeds

3 tablespoons vegetable oil

1 yellow onion, chopped

3 carrots, chopped

3 celery stalks, chopped, leaves reserved if bright green

Kosher salt

1 teaspoon ancho chili powder

1 teaspoon chipotle chili powder

1 teaspoon guajillo chili powder

4 cups chicken broth

1 cup canned diced tomatoes

1 smoked chicken carcass (optional)

½ of a smoked chicken, meat pulled off the bone and chopped

3 corn tortillas, cut into strips

This is no ordinary chicken-tortilla soup. When you're starting with barbecued chicken, there's no way it can be ordinary. Customize each bowl with your favorite toppings, like sour cream, chopped onion, chopped cilantro, or lime juice, for the perfect balance of flavors in every bite.

**1.** In a large pot, heat the cumin seeds in the oil over medium heat for 3 to 4 minutes, or until fragrant.

**2.** Increase the heat to medium high and add the onion, carrots, and celery. Cook for 6 to 7 minutes, or until slightly softened.

**3.** Season with salt and add the ancho chili powder, chipotle chili powder, guajillo chili powder, chicken broth, tomatoes, celery leaves (if using), and chicken carcass (if using).

**4.** Bring to a simmer and cook for 15 to 20 minutes, or until the vegetables are tender.

**5.** Add the chopped meat and simmer for 3 to 4 minutes to allow the flavors to meld.

**6.** Add the tortilla strips and simmer for about 1 minute, or until softened.

**7.** Divide among 8 bowls and serve immediately.

**PAIR IT** This soup goes great with the Tried-and-True Kale Salad (page 141).

# GLAZED CHICKEN QUARTERS

**SERVES 6**

PREP TIME: 30 MINUTES

COOK TIME: 2½ TO 3 HOURS

RECOMMENDED WOOD: PECAN

6 chicken quarters

⅓ cup "Good on Everything" Dry Rub (page 121)

1 cup Mild Barbecue Sauce (page 112)

2 tablespoons vegetable oil, plus more for brushing the grates

This recipe is a bit more work, but it's definitely worthwhile. Brushing on barbecue sauce creates a nice glaze in the last 15 to 20 minutes in the smoker and adds another layer of flavor.

1. Soak 4½ cups of wood chips in water for 15 to 30 minutes.

2. Wash the chicken and pat it dry. Let it come to room temperature.

3. Preheat the smoker to 225°F to 250°F and add the wood chips, following the manufacturer's instructions.

4. If the grates haven't been oiled: Roll up a clean, lint-free kitchen towel and dip it into some vegetable oil. Using tongs, grab the towel and rub it across the grates.

5. Coat the chicken thoroughly in the dry rub and place it on the grates in a single layer.

6. Close the cooking compartment and smoke for 2¼ to 2¾ hours. Soak additional wood chips and replenish as needed; if you no longer see smoke exiting the chimneys or vents, add more wood.

7. Remove the chicken from the smoker. In a large sauté pan, heat the 2 tablespoons of vegetable oil over high heat. When the oil is hot, brown the chicken on each side for 1½ to 2 minutes, or until the skin is crisp.

8. Brush the barbecue sauce all over the chicken and return the chicken to the smoker for 15 to 20 minutes, or until an instant-read thermometer inserted into the flesh without touching the bone reads at least 160°F. Let the chicken rest for 5 minutes before serving.

# BRINED, BACON-WRAPPED CHICKEN BREASTS

**SERVES 6**

PREP TIME: 1 ½ HOURS

COOK TIME: 2 TO 2 ½ HOURS

RECOMMENDED WOOD: APPLE

6 boneless, skinless chicken breasts

8 cups All-Purpose Brine (page 126)

Vegetable oil, for brushing the grates

1 pound bacon

Boneless, skinless chicken breasts have a reputation for being a bit dry when cooked. However, brining them and wrapping them in bacon will keep them moist and flavorful as they smoke. When shopping for chicken breasts, look for ones that are of similar weights so they will finish cooking at the same time.

1. In a nonreactive container, submerge the chicken in the brine for 1 to 1 ½ hours.

2. Soak 3 cups of wood chips in water for 15 to 30 minutes.

3. Pat the chicken dry and let it come to room temperature.

4. Preheat the smoker to 225°F to 250°F and add the wood chips, following the manufacturer's instructions.

5. If the grates haven't been oiled: Roll up a clean, lint-free kitchen towel and dip it into some vegetable oil. Using tongs, grab the towel and rub it across the grates. Wrap the breasts with the bacon and place them on the grates in a single layer.

6. Close the cooking compartment and smoke for 2 to 2 ½ hours, or until an instant-read thermometer inserted into the flesh reads at least 160°F. Soak additional wood chips and replenish as needed; if you no longer see smoke exiting the chimneys or vents, add more wood.

7. Let the chicken rest for 5 minutes before serving.

**TROUBLESHOOTING** Make sure to cool the brine completely before using.

# SMOKED TURKEY LEGS

**SERVES 6 TO 8**

PREP TIME: 3 TO 4 HOURS

COOK TIME: 4 HOURS

RECOMMENDED WOOD: APPLE

6 turkey legs

1 gallon Apple Juice Brine
(page 127)

½ cup "Good on Everything"
Dry Rub (page 121)

2 tablespoons vegetable oil,
plus more for brushing
the grates

There's something whimsical about picking up a giant turkey leg at the dinner table and gnawing on it. Maybe it makes you feel like you're at a jousting match in medieval times or a king at a royal feast. Don't forget the chalice of mead.

**1.** In a nonreactive container, submerge the turkey in the brine for 3 to 4 hours.

**2.** Soak 6 cups of wood chips in water for 15 to 30 minutes.

**3.** Pat the turkey dry and let it come to room temperature.

**4.** Preheat the smoker to 225°F to 250°F and add the wood chips, following the manufacturer's instructions.

**5.** If the grates haven't been oiled: Roll up a clean, lint-free kitchen towel and dip it into some vegetable oil. Using tongs, grab the towel and rub it across the grates.

**6.** Coat the legs thoroughly in the dry rub and place them on the grates in a single layer.

**7.** Close the cooking compartment and smoke for about 4 hours, or until an instant-read thermometer inserted into the flesh without touching the bone reads at least 160°F. Soak additional wood chips and replenish as needed; if you no longer see smoke exiting the chimneys or vents, add more wood.

**8.** In a large sauté pan, heat the 2 tablespoons of vegetable oil over high heat. When the oil is hot, add the turkey and brown on each side for 1½ to 2 minutes, or until the skin is crisp. Let the turkey rest for 10 minutes before serving.

# SMOKED TURKEY BREASTS

**SERVES 6**

PREP TIME: 30 MINUTES,
PLUS OVERNIGHT TO BRINE

COOK TIME: 4 TO 6 HOURS

RECOMMENDED WOOD: ORANGE

1 bone-in, skin-on turkey breast

1 gallon Citrus Brine (page 129)

⅓ cup "Good on Everything"
Dry Rub (page 121)

2 tablespoons vegetable oil,
plus more for brushing
the grates

If you're hosting a smaller Thanksgiving get-together this year, consider smoking turkey breasts, which are large enough to feed six people each. Brining them renders them juicy and flavorful, while the dry rub results in tasty skin.

1. In a nonreactive container, submerge the turkey in the brine overnight.

2. Soak 9 cups of wood chips in water for 15 to 30 minutes.

3. Pat the turkey dry and let it come to room temperature.

4. Preheat the smoker to 225°F to 250°F and add the wood chips, following the manufacturer's instructions.

5. If the grates haven't been oiled: Roll up a clean, lint-free kitchen towel and dip it into some vegetable oil. Using tongs, grab the towel and rub it across the grates.

6. Coat the turkey thoroughly in the dry rub and place it on the grates.

7. Close the cooking compartment and smoke for 4 to 6 hours, or until an instant-read thermometer inserted into the flesh without touching the bone reads at least 160°F. Soak additional wood chips and replenish as needed; if you no longer see smoke exiting the chimneys or vents, add more wood.

8. In a large sauté pan, heat the 2 tablespoons of vegetable oil over high heat. When the oil is hot, add the turkey and brown skin-side down for 1½ to 2 minutes, or until the skin is crisp. Let the turkey rest for 10 minutes before serving.

**TROUBLESHOOTING** To help the breasts stay submerged in the brine, use plates or clean bricks to weigh them down.

# SMOKED THANKSGIVING TURKEY

**SERVES 10 TO 12**

PREP TIME: 30 MINUTES,
PLUS OVERNIGHT TO BRINE

COOK TIME: 6½ HOURS

RECOMMENDED WOOD: PECAN

1 (12-pound) turkey

2 gallons All-Purpose Brine
(page 126)

½ cup "Good on Everything"
Dry Rub (page 121)

2 tablespoons vegetable oil,
plus more for brushing
the grates

When Thanksgiving comes, people either stick to tradition and never waver or go on the hunt (again) for the turkey recipe to end all recipes—or at least one that promises a juicier, tastier bird. Well, here's one that might just become tradition.

**1.** In a nonreactive container, submerge the turkey in the brine overnight.

**2.** Soak 12 cups of wood chips in water for 15 to 30 minutes.

**3.** Pat the turkey dry and let it come to room temperature.

**4.** Preheat the smoker to 225°F to 250°F and add the wood chips, following the manufacturer's instructions.

**5.** If the grates haven't been oiled: Roll up a clean, lint-free kitchen towel and dip it into some vegetable oil. Using tongs, grab the towel and rub it across the grates.

**6.** Coat the turkey thoroughly in the dry rub and place it breast-side up on the grates.

**7.** Close the cooking compartment and smoke for about 6½ hours, or until an instant-read thermometer inserted into the flesh without touching the bone reads at least 160°F. Soak additional wood chips and replenish as needed; if you no longer see smoke exiting the chimneys or vents, add more wood.

**8.** In a large sauté pan, heat the 2 tablespoons of vegetable oil over high heat. When the oil is hot, add the turkey and brown for 1½ to 2 minutes on each side, or until the skin is crisp. Let the turkey rest for 20 minutes before serving.

**SMOKING TIP** Bringing proteins to room temperature before smoking results in even cooking.

# SMOKED SPATCHCOCKED CHICKEN

**SERVES 4 TO 6**

PREP TIME: 30 MINUTES

COOK TIME: 2 ½ TO 3 HOURS

RECOMMENDED WOOD: PECAN

1 whole chicken

⅓ cup "Good on Everything" Dry Rub (page 121)

2 tablespoons vegetable oil, plus more for brushing the grates

Spatchcocking, or flattening, the chicken allows you to coat the interior with dry rub.

**1.** Soak 4½ cups of wood chips in water for 15 to 30 minutes.

**2.** Wash the chicken and pat it dry. Let it come to room temperature.

**3.** Preheat the smoker to 225°F to 250°F and add the wood chips, following the manufacturer's instructions.

**4.** If the grates haven't been oiled: Roll up a clean, lint-free kitchen towel and dip it into some vegetable oil. Using tongs, grab the towel and rub it across the grates.

**5.** Place the chicken breast-side down on a cutting board. Using kitchen scissors, cut down along both sides of the backbone. Open up the chicken and, using a sharp knife, make shallow cuts along the bone that runs down the center of the breast. Flip the bird over and, using both palms, press down on the breast until it cracks.

**6.** Coat the chicken thoroughly in the dry rub and place it breast-side up on the grates.

**7.** Close the cooking compartment and smoke for about 2½ to 3 hours, or until an instant-read thermometer inserted into the flesh without touching the bone reads at least 160°F. Soak additional wood chips and replenish as needed; if you no longer see smoke exiting the chimneys or vents, add more wood.

**8.** In a large sauté pan, heat the 2 tablespoons of vegetable oil over high heat. When the oil is hot, add the chicken, breast-side down, and brown it for 1½ to 2 minutes, or until the skin is crisp. Let the chicken rest for 10 minutes before serving.

# BEER CAN CHICKEN

**SERVES 4**

PREP TIME: 30 MINUTES

COOK TIME: 3 TO 4 HOURS

RECOMMENDED WOOD: PECAN

1 whole chicken

⅓ cup "Good on Everything" Dry Rub (page 121)

1 can American lager, such as Budweiser, half empty

2 tablespoons vegetable oil, plus more for brushing the grates

Beer can chicken is sheer genius, and a classic. The beer evaporates and moistens the interior as the chicken cooks, making the meat juicy.

**1.** Soak 3 cups of wood chips in water for 15 to 30 minutes.

**2.** Wash the chicken and pat it dry. Let it come to room temperature.

**3.** Preheat the smoker to 225°F to 250°F and add the wood chips, following the manufacturer's instructions.

**4.** If the grates haven't been oiled: Roll up a clean, lint-free kitchen towel and dip it into some vegetable oil. Using tongs, grab the towel and rub it across the grates.

**5.** Coat the chicken thoroughly in the dry rub and insert the beer can, right-side up, into the cavity. Using the beer can and legs as a three-point stand, place the chicken on the grates, wings facing up.

**6.** Close the cooking compartment and smoke for about 3 to 4 hours, or until an instant-read thermometer inserted into the flesh without touching the bone reads at least 160°F. Soak additional wood chips and replenish as needed; if you no longer see smoke exiting the chimneys or vents, add more wood.

**7.** In a large sauté pan, heat the 2 tablespoons of vegetable oil over high heat. When the oil is hot, add the chicken and brown on each side for 1½ to 2 minutes, or until the skin is crisp. Let the chicken rest for 20 minutes before serving.

**TROUBLESHOOTING** If the chicken refuses to stand, open up a couple more cans, drink some of the beer, and use them to prop it up.

## CHAPTER FOUR

# PORK

In Memphis and the Carolinas, nothing gets the heart of a barbecue fanatic beating faster than the smell of barbecued pork wafting through the air. In fact, out there, pork *is* barbecue; there's nothing else that deserves the name. In this chapter, you'll learn to prepare the various popular cuts to perfection. 🐖

# TECHNIQUES

If you cooked your way through the poultry chapter, you'll find the techniques used on pork mostly familiar. In a way, you can think of chicken as your barbecue training wheels: It's a small, cheap, and quick-cooking animal (well, about as quick as you can make barbecue). So even if you mess up, it isn't the end of the world.

Now it's time to take off the training wheels. In this chapter, you'll use dry rubs to create the primary layer of flavor on every cut, from ribs to loins and shoulders. You'll also use marinades and brines to help infuse additional flavor into the meat.

Brines are especially important for lean cuts like pork loin, which comes from the animal's back. The loin is very tender and lends itself to long, slow cooking processes like roasting and (of course) smoking. But it has a tendency to dry out, which means that getting the brine to penetrate into as much of the flesh as possible is very important. The best way to achieve this is by injecting the brine.

You'll need a kitchen syringe (available at home goods stores, barbecue supply stores, and sometimes supermarkets; look near the turkey basters) and a strainer. The brine needs to be strained before injecting it into the meat to make sure that any herbs, spices, or other ingredients don't clog the syringe. Before using the syringe, remove the plunger and apply a small amount of vegetable oil to the seal so that the plunger slides up and down easily. Fill up the syringe and inject equal amounts of the brine at evenly spaced intervals throughout the flesh; 5 cc's an inch apart works pretty well, but go ahead and experiment.

A few recipes in this chapter deal with baby back and spare ribs. On the back side of the ribs, you'll find a membrane. It's really up to you whether you want to remove it or not. If you don't, it will help hold the ribs together as they cook, which makes them easier to pick up. However, some people think the membrane makes ribs harder to eat and say that it keeps dry rubs from being absorbed all the way through the meat. If you decide to remove the membrane, start at a corner, and work the tip of a sharp paring knife underneath it. Gently pull up, and grasp it between your thumb and forefinger while pulling firmly away.

The USDA-recommended internal temperature for cooked pork is 145°F. This is fine for lean cuts like loin and chops. But traditional barbecue cuts like ribs and shoulders don't turn tender until well past 145°F. In fact, ribs don't pull apart easily until between 175°F and 190°F, and shoulders aren't at their best until about 185°F to 205°F, temperatures at which leaner cuts would be overcooked and dry. At lower temperatures, the collagen in the connective tissue hasn't broken down into gelatin, which is what gives that silky mouthfeel that's the sign of good barbecue. So, as always, if you want it to be good, you'll have to be patient. Use an instant-read thermometer inserted into the thickest part of the meat without touching the bone to keep a constant read on the internal temperature.

NEED-TO-KNOW TIPS

**No shiners.** When buying ribs, examine the surface of the meat carefully. If you see any patches of white, ask for another rack. These visible patches of bone indicate that the meat was not butchered properly.

**Avoid cross-contamination.** Use a separate, nonporous cutting board for prepping raw pork.

**Brining? Be cool.** Brines should be refrigerated before using. Don't pour boiling brine over raw meat.

**Be smart with marinades.** If you plan on using a marinade to baste the skin periodically as the pork cooks in the smoker, or to use it as a sauce, bring it to a boil first to kill any harmful bacteria.

**Let it rest.** Now that you're working with larger cuts from a larger animal, it's especially important to let the meat rest before slicing into it. This will allow the juices to redistribute throughout the meat instead of leaking all over your cutting board. After all, if you've already waited several hours (or a whole day!) for your meat to smoke, what's another 30 minutes if it means all your hard work won't go to waste?

# WINNER-TAKE-ALL BABY BACK RIBS

**SERVES 4**

PREP TIME: 30 MINUTES

COOK TIME: 4 TO 5 HOURS

RECOMMENDED WOOD:
APPLE OR CHERRY

2 racks baby back ribs

Vegetable oil, for brushing
the grates

⅔ cup "Good on Everything"
Dry Rub (page 121)

These ribs come out so tasty that you don't even need to think about putting sauce on them. The dry rub really brings out the natural flavor of the pork. Use the best quality meat that you can find—antibiotic-free and organic, or heirloom breed, if you can get it.

1. Soak 6 cups of wood chips in water for 15 to 30 minutes.

2. Bring the ribs to room temperature.

3. Preheat the smoker to 200°F to 225°F and add the wood chips, following the manufacturer's instructions.

4. If the grates haven't been oiled: Roll up a clean, lint-free kitchen towel and dip it into some vegetable oil. Using tongs, grab the towel and rub it across the grates.

5. Coat the ribs thoroughly in the dry rub and place them on the grates.

6. Close the cooking compartment and smoke for 4 to 5 hours, or until the ribs pull apart easily. Soak additional wood chips and replenish as needed; if you no longer see smoke exiting the chimneys or vents, add more wood.

7. Let the ribs rest for 10 minutes before serving.

**PAIR IT** If you absolutely must have sauce, serve some Mild Barbecue Sauce (page 112) or Kansas City–Style Barbecue Sauce (page 111) on the side.

# "BIG AS TEXAS" SPARE RIBS

**SERVES 6**

PREP TIME: 30 MINUTES

COOK TIME: 6 HOURS

RECOMMENDED WOOD: HICKORY

2 racks St. Louis–style spare ribs

Vegetable oil, for brushing the grates

⅔ cup Texas Dry Rub (page 125)

Texans are typically all about beef when it comes to barbecue, but every once in a while they get an inexplicable craving for pork. And when they do, they get a nice rack of spare ribs, coat them with a bit of smoky dry rub, and cook them low and slow.

1. Soak 9 cups of wood chips in water for 15 to 30 minutes.

2. Bring the ribs to room temperature.

3. Preheat the smoker to 200°F to 225°F and add the wood chips, following the manufacturer's instructions.

4. If the grates haven't been oiled: Roll up a clean, lint-free kitchen towel and dip it into some vegetable oil. Using tongs, grab the towel and rub it across the grates.

5. Coat the ribs thoroughly in the dry rub and place them on the grates.

6. Close the cooking compartment and smoke for about 6 hours, or until the ribs pull apart easily. Soak additional wood chips and replenish as needed; if you no longer see smoke exiting the chimneys or vents, add more wood.

7. Let the ribs rest for 10 minutes before serving.

**SMOKING TIP** St. Louis–style spare ribs are just regular spare ribs that have been trimmed into a rectangular shape, which is better for smoking since they cook more evenly.

# KANSAS CITY–STYLE GLAZED SPARE RIBS

**SERVES 6**

PREP TIME: 30 MINUTES

COOK TIME: 6 HOURS

RECOMMENDED WOOD:
APPLE OR CHERRY

2 racks St. Louis–style spare ribs

Vegetable oil, for brushing
the grates

⅔ cup "Good on Everything"
Dry Rub (page 121)

1 cup Kansas City–Style
Barbecue Sauce (page 111)

In Kansas City, they love pork spare ribs just as much as they love beef brisket. And they love using dry rubs just as much as they do sauce, which is why they usually use both when smoking ribs to create a double layer of flavor.

1. Soak 9 cups of wood chips in water for 15 to 30 minutes.

2. Bring the ribs to room temperature.

3. Preheat the smoker to 200°F to 225°F and add the wood chips, following the manufacturer's instructions.

4. If the grates haven't been oiled: Roll up a clean, lint-free kitchen towel and dip it into some vegetable oil. Using tongs, grab the towel and rub it across the grates.

5. Coat the ribs thoroughly in the dry rub and place them on the grates.

6. Close the cooking compartment and smoke for about 6 hours, or until the ribs pull apart easily. Soak additional wood chips and replenish as needed; if you no longer see smoke exiting the chimneys or vents, add more wood.

7. In the last 15 to 20 minutes of cooking, quickly brush the barbecue sauce all over the ribs.

8. Let the ribs rest for 10 minutes before serving.

**SMOKING TIP** If you decide to brush sauce on your barbecue, do so in the last 15 to 20 minutes of cooking to keep the sugars in it from burning.

# HICKORY-SMOKED PORK BELLY

**SERVES 8**

PREP TIME: 30 MINUTES,
PLUS OVERNIGHT TO BRINE

COOK TIME: 2 TO 2 ½ HOURS

RECOMMENDED WOOD: HICKORY

1 pork belly

4 cups Apple Juice Brine
(page 127)

Vegetable oil, for brushing
the grates

½ cup Coffee-Chili Dry Rub
(page 120)

The bold, savory flavor of hickory matches up perfectly with the intense richness of pork belly. You probably know pork belly by another name: bacon. Bacon is what you get when you cold smoke pork belly. Here, you'll be hot smoking it, or barbecuing it, with equally delicious results.

1. In a nonreactive container, submerge the pork belly in the brine overnight.

2. Soak 3 cups of hickory wood chips in water for 15 to 30 minutes.

3. Pat the pork belly dry and let them come to room temperature.

4. Preheat the smoker to 200°F to 225°F and add the wood chips, following the manufacturer's instructions.

5. If the grates haven't been oiled: Roll up a clean, lint-free kitchen towel and dip it into some vegetable oil. Using tongs, grab the towel and rub it across the grates.

6. Coat the pork belly thoroughly in the dry rub and place it on the grates.

7. Close the cooking compartment and smoke for 2 to 2½ hours, or until an instant-read thermometer inserted into the flesh reads at least 140°F. Soak additional wood chips and replenish as needed; if you no longer see smoke exiting the chimneys or vents, add more wood.

8. Let the pork rest for 15 minutes before serving.

# SUNDAY DINNER PORK LOIN

**SERVES 18 TO 20**

PREP TIME: 30 MINUTES,
PLUS OVERNIGHT TO BRINE

COOK TIME: 3 ½ TO 4 HOURS

RECOMMENDED WOOD: APPLE

1 (7- to 8-pound) pork loin

1 gallon Apple Juice Brine
(page 127)

Vegetable oil, for brushing
the grates

1 cup "Good on Everything"
Dry Rub (page 121)

Pork loin is not a traditional cut for barbecue because it is very lean. However, if brined overnight, it remains juicy and flavorful during the smoking process, and it's quick-cooking for its size.

**1.** In a nonreactive container, submerge the pork loin in the brine overnight.

**2.** Soak 6 cups of wood chips in water for 15 to 30 minutes.

**3.** Pat the pork loin dry and let it come to room temperature.

**4.** Strain the brine and use a kitchen syringe to inject the brine at evenly spaced intervals throughout the loin.

**5.** Preheat the smoker to 200°F to 225°F and add the wood chips, following the manufacturer's instructions.

**6.** If the grates haven't been oiled: Roll up a clean, lint-free kitchen towel and dip it into some vegetable oil. Using tongs, grab the towel and rub it across the grates.

**7.** Coat the loin thoroughly in the dry rub and place it on the grates.

**8.** Close the cooking compartment and smoke for 3½ to 4 hours, or until an instant-read thermometer inserted into the flesh reads at least 140°F. Soak additional wood chips and replenish as needed; if you no longer see smoke exiting the chimneys or vents, add more wood.

**9.** Let the pork rest for 20 minutes before serving.

**SMOKING TIP** Because the loin is such a large, uniform cut, it gives the perfect opportunity to experiment. Try rubbing different portions of the loin with different dry rubs.

# BEER-MARINATED BOSTON BUTT

**SERVES 18 TO 20**

PREP TIME: 30 MINUTES,
PLUS OVERNIGHT TO MARINATE

COOK TIME: 10 ½ TO 12 HOURS

RECOMMENDED WOOD:
APPLE OR CHERRY

1 (7- to 8-pound) Boston butt

1 gallon Beer Marinade
(page 128)

Vegetable oil, for brushing
the grates

1 cup "Good on Everything"
Dry Rub (page 121)

Boston butt, or pork butt, is actually part of the animal's shoulder, not its hindquarters, as one might assume. The cut includes the bone, which imparts great flavor. Although smoking one takes a long while, the end result is well worth the wait.

1. In a nonreactive container, submerge the pork butt in the marinade overnight.

2. Soak 4½ quarts of wood chips in water for 15 to 30 minutes.

3. Pat the pork butt dry and let it come to room temperature.

4. Preheat the smoker to 200°F to 225°F and add the wood chips, following the manufacturer's instructions.

5. If the grates haven't been oiled: Roll up a clean, lint-free kitchen towel and dip it into some vegetable oil. Using tongs, grab the towel and rub it across the grates.

6. Coat the pork butt thoroughly in the dry rub and place it on the grates.

7. Close the cooking compartment and smoke for 10½ to 12 hours, or until an instant-read thermometer inserted into the flesh reads at least 205°F. Soak additional wood chips and replenish as needed; if you no longer see smoke exiting the chimneys or vents, add more wood.

8. Let the pork rest for 20 minutes before serving. Use 2 forks to pull apart the meat.

**SMOKING TIP** Rich, fatty cuts with a lot of connective tissue, like pork butt, need extra time to turn succulent, which is why the recommended internal temperature is far above USDA guidelines. It will not taste overcooked.

# CAROLINA-STYLE PICNIC SHOULDER

**SERVES 18 TO 20**

PREP TIME: 30 MINUTES,
PLUS OVERNIGHT TO BRINE

COOK TIME: 10½ TO 12 HOURS

RECOMMENDED WOOD:
APPLE OR CHERRY

1 (7- to 8-pound) picnic
shoulder

1 gallon Apple Juice Brine
(page 127)

Vegetable oil, for brushing
the grates

1 cup "Good on Everything"
Dry Rub (page 121)

The picnic shoulder, or picnic ham, is another part of the shoulder that can be used to make pulled pork. This cut is boneless, which is why it's injected with brine to keep it from drying out as it cooks.

**1.** In a nonreactive container, submerge the pork picnic shoulder in the marinade overnight.

**2.** Soak 4½ quarts of wood chips in water for 15 to 30 minutes.

**3.** Pat the picnic shoulder dry and let it come to room temperature.

**4.** Strain the brine and use a kitchen syringe to inject the brine at evenly spaced intervals throughout the picnic shoulder.

**5.** Preheat the smoker to 200°F to 225°F and add the wood chips, following the manufacturer's instructions.

**6.** If the grates haven't been oiled: Roll up a clean, lint-free kitchen towel and dip it into some vegetable oil. Using tongs, grab the towel and rub it across the grates.

**7.** Coat the shoulder thoroughly in the dry rub and place it on the grates.

**8.** Close the cooking compartment and smoke for 10½ to 12 hours, or until an instant-read thermometer inserted into the flesh reads at least 205°F. Soak additional wood chips and replenish as needed; if you no longer see smoke exiting the chimneys or vents, add more wood.

**9.** Let the pork rest for 20 minutes before serving. Use 2 forks to pull apart the meat.

**PAIR IT** Serve with Spicy Carolina-Style Vinegar Sauce (page 117) or Spicy Carolina-Style Mustard Sauce (page 116).

# "WHOLE LOTTA LOVE" PORK SHOULDER

**SERVES 32 TO 48**

PREP TIME: 30 MINUTES

COOK TIME: 18 TO 27 HOURS

RECOMMENDED WOOD:
APPLE OR CHERRY

**1 (12- to 18-pound) whole pork shoulder**

**Vegetable oil, for brushing the grates**

**2 cups "Good on Everything" Dry Rub (page 121)**

This recipe is perfect for those who like a challenge and want to move beyond just smoking pork butts or picnic shoulders. It's the whole shoulder, so it's huge. Expect all-day and all-night cooking requiring shifts at the smoker (unless yours is electric), but when everything's done, you'll be able to feed the whole street.

**1.** Soak 4½ quarts of wood chips in water for 15 to 30 minutes.

**2.** Bring the pork shoulder to room temperature.

**3.** Preheat the smoker to 200°F to 225°F and add the wood chips, following the manufacturer's instructions.

**4.** If the grates haven't been oiled: Roll up a clean, lint-free kitchen towel and dip it into some vegetable oil. Using tongs, grab the towel and rub it across the grates.

**5.** Coat the shoulder thoroughly in the dry rub and place it on the grates.

**6.** Close the cooking compartment and smoke for 18 to 27 hours, or until an instant-read thermometer inserted into the flesh without touching the bone reads at least 205°F. Soak additional wood chips and replenish as needed; if you no longer see smoke exiting the chimneys or vents, add more wood.

**7.** Let the pork rest for 30 to 45 minutes before serving. Use 2 forks to pull apart the meat.

**SMOKING TIP** For longer smoke jobs, try a combination of wood chips and chunks. Chips will provide a lot of initial smoke, while chunks will go through a slow burn to keep a steady level of smoke going later on.

# PULLED PORK SANDWICHES WITH TANGY SLAW

**SERVES 4**

PREP TIME: 5 MINUTES

4 brioche rolls, split

4 cups pulled pork from Beer-Marinated Boston Butt (page 61) or Carolina-Style Picnic Shoulder (page 62)

2 cups Simple Cole Slaw (page 138)

¼ cup Spicy Carolina-Style Vinegar Sauce (page 117)

There's no such thing as just a little bit of pulled pork. So if you're wondering what to do with all that meat, these sandwiches are a great way to perk up your weekday lunch routine or to bring on a picnic nearby.

**1.** On the heel of each bun, place one-quarter of the pulled pork. Top with coleslaw.

**2.** Drizzle the Vinegar Sauce over the coleslaw, and top with the crown of the bun.

**PAIR IT** To turn this into a complete meal, serve the sandwiches with some Wild West Baked Beans (page 156).

# PULLED PORK TACOS WITH SALSA VERDE

PREP TIME: 10 MINUTES

4 cups pulled pork from
Beer-Marinated Boston Butt
(page 61) or Carolina-Style
Picnic Shoulder (page 62)

12 corn tortillas

1 cup Salsa Verde (page 113)

½ cup chopped yellow onion

½ cup chopped fresh cilantro

Here's another great way to work a little bit of pulled pork magic into your everyday favorites. A simple salsa verde contrasts wonderfully with the richness of the pork, and bit of chopped onion provides some crunch with every bite.

**1.** Divide the meat evenly among the tortillas.

**2.** Top with the Salsa Verde, yellow onion, and cilantro. Serve immediately.

**PAIR IT** A light Mexican lager such as Modelo Especial would be perfect with these tacos.

# BEEF

In the heart of Texas, barbecue is beef by definition. There is a long tradition of smoking beef that goes back to the days when Mexican cowboys would settle down at the end of a long, hard week and slow-cook the head of a steer in a pit in the ground to create a delicious treat called barbacoa. That tradition is carried on today in some parts of Texas.

The German immigrants of South Carolina began different traditions in their butcher shops. When all the choicest cuts were sold by the day's end, they were left only with the incredibly tough brisket. Out of necessity, they learned to transform this undesirable cut of beef into delicious eats by cooking it low and slow with smoke.

While brisket is arguably the pillar of modern beef barbecue, these days pitmasters have begun to experiment with smoking nontraditional cuts like prime rib and tenderloin. You'll have a chance to work with it all in this chapter.

## TECHNIQUES

Brining, marinating, and injecting aren't really necessary when you're barbecuing beef. The recipes here require a simple dry rub, and then the meat goes right into the smoker. The challenge lies in hitting the right temperatures and maintaining consistency.

Getting the temperature right depends on the cut of beef you're barbecuing. A traditional barbecue cut like brisket, for example, has a lot of fat and connective tissue, so it reaches its melt-in-your-mouth best at 195°F or even higher. Pull it out early, and you'll end up with chewy meat. Leaner cuts, like a tenderloin or prime rib, are best served rare or medium rare, so shoot for 125°F to 130°F. They'll turn tough, just like an overcooked steak, if they spend more time than necessary in the smoker. If you're working with ground meat, as in meatballs or meatloaf, cook to the USDA-recommended internal temperature of 160°F.

To avoid temperature fluctuations, especially with long cook times, there are three things you will need: a thermometer with a remote probe, which allows you to monitor the meat's temperature without opening the smoking compartment; enough wood on hand to maintain sufficient smoke throughout the cooking process; and enough fuel to maintain the heat. If you're using wood chips for smoke, plan on adding about 1 to 1½ cups every hour. If you're using a charcoal smoker, plan on using about 15 pieces of charcoal an hour. A 20-pound propane tank yields 30 hours of cooking.

# SMOKED BEEF SAUSAGES

**SERVES 4**

PREP TIME: 30 MINUTES

COOK TIME: 2 HOURS

RECOMMENDED WOOD:
OAK OR HICKORY

**4 beef bratwursts**

**Vegetable oil, for brushing the grates**

Sure, you could leave the smoking up to the professionals and buy presmoked sausages, but what would be the fun in that? Smoking your own sausage allows you to put your personal stamp on it. Create your own blend of hardwoods to give your sausage a unique flavor and aroma.

**1.** Soak 3 cups of wood chips in water for 15 to 30 minutes.

**2.** Bring the sausages to room temperature.

**3.** Preheat the smoker to 225°F to 240°F and add the wood chips, following the manufacturer's instructions.

**4.** If the grates haven't been oiled: Roll up a clean, lint-free kitchen towel and dip it into some vegetable oil. Using tongs, grab the towel and rub it across the grates.

**5.** Place the sausages on the grates in a single layer.

**6.** Close the cooking compartment and smoke for about 2 hours. Soak additional wood chips and replenish as needed; if you no longer see smoke exiting the chimneys or vents, add more wood.

**7.** Serve immediately.

# HOME RUN HOT DOGS

**SERVES 4**

PREP TIME: 5 MINUTES

4 hot dog buns, split

4 Smoked Beef Sausages
(page 69)

2 tablespoons Mild Barbecue
Sauce (page 112)

2 tablespoons yellow mustard

¼ cup chopped yellow onion

While it's easy to get a bit nostalgic over ballpark hot dogs, if you're truly honest with yourself, they're usually not that great. These hot dogs, however, are real winners. After all, if you're smoking your own sausages, you really can't do any better.

1. In a dry skillet over high heat, toast the hot dog buns cut-side down for 30 seconds to 1 minute.

2. Place the sausages in the buns and top with the barbecue sauce, mustard, and onion. Serve immediately.

# SMOKED MEATBALLS

SERVES 4

PREP TIME: 30 MINUTES

COOK TIME: 1 ½ TO 2 HOURS

RECOMMENDED WOOD:
OAK OR HICKORY

1¾ pounds 85/15 ground beef

2 large eggs

1⅓ cups fresh breadcrumbs

Kosher salt

Freshly ground black pepper

Sure, you've had them baked, simmered, and perhaps even fried, but have you ever had meatballs smoked? If not, it's time to give them a try. These are delicious all on their own as a snack, or served with some cooked pasta as a complete meal.

**1.** Soak 3 cups of wood chips in water for 15 to 30 minutes.

**2.** Preheat the smoker to 250°F and add the wood chips, following the manufacturer's instructions.

**3.** In a large bowl, add the beef, eggs, and breadcrumbs. Season with salt and pepper, and mix using your hands just until loosely combined.

**4.** Form the meat into 1-inch balls and place the meatballs on a sheet pan or disposable aluminum pan. Place the pan on the grates.

**5.** Close the cooking compartment and smoke for 1 ½ to 2 hours, or until an instant-read thermometer inserted into a meatball reads at least 160°F. Soak additional wood chips and replenish as needed; if you no longer see smoke exiting the chimneys or vents, add more wood.

**6.** Let the meatballs rest for 5 minutes before serving.

# KNOCKOUT MEATBALL PARM

**SERVES 4**

PREP TIME: 15 MINUTES

COOK TIME: 5 MINUTES

2 pounds Smoked Meatballs
(page 71)

4 (12-inch) sub rolls, split

1½ cups Smoky Tomato Sauce
(page 115)

½ pound fresh whole-milk
mozzarella, sliced

½ cup grated hard Italian
cheese, preferably Parmigiano-
Reggiano or Grana Padano

This is not your average meatball parm. A smoky tomato sauce with hints of cumin and super-savory smoked meatballs create a flavor sensation that won't be soon forgotten. Use the highest quality mozzarella you can find, preferably sitting in liquid and freshly made that day.

**1.** Preheat the oven to 450°F.

**2.** Divide the meatballs evenly among the rolls and top them with the tomato sauce, mozzarella, and Parmesan cheese.

**3.** Place the sandwiches on a baking sheet and transfer them to the oven for 2 to 3 minutes, or until the sauce is bubbly and the cheese is melted.

**PAIR IT** Want to indulge in a meatball parm but prefer to lighten things up a bit? Split one with a friend and whip up a side of Radish and Beet Salad with Basil (page 145). It's cool, crunchy, and tangy, the perfect contrast to these rich meatball subs.

# HOLIDAY PRIME RIB

**SERVES 32 TO 48**

PREP TIME: 30 MINUTES

COOK TIME: 5 HOURS

RECOMMENDED WOOD:
OAK OR HICKORY

1 (5-pound) prime rib

Vegetable oil, for brushing
the grates

¾ cup "Good on Everything"
Dry Rub (page 121)

If you're fortunate enough to live in an area where outdoor cooking is still an option during the winter months, then you may want to try something different with the holiday roast. Prime rib (also called standing rib roast) takes on a beautiful crust as it cooks in the smoker, while the interior turns a perfect rosy pink, yielding flesh that is juicy and flavorful.

1. Soak 7½ cups of wood chips in water for 15 to 30 minutes.

2. Bring the prime rib to room temperature.

3. Preheat the smoker to 225°F to 240°F and add the wood chips, following the manufacturer's instructions.

4. If the grates haven't been oiled: Roll up a clean, lint-free kitchen towel and dip it into some vegetable oil. Using tongs, grab the towel and rub it across the grates.

5. Using strips of butcher's twine and going in the same direction as the bones, tie up the prime rib in 1-inch intervals.

6. Coat the prime rib thoroughly in the dry rub and place it on the grates.

7. Close the cooking compartment and smoke for about 5 hours, or until an instant-read thermometer inserted into the flesh without touching the bone reads 130°F. Soak additional wood chips and replenish as needed; if you no longer see smoke exiting the chimneys or vents, add more wood.

8. Let the prime rib rest for 30 to 45 minutes before serving. Slice in between the bones or carve off the bones entirely, and slice against the grain.

# SMOKIN' CHUCK ROAST

**SERVES 14 TO 18**

PREP TIME: 30 MINUTES

COOK TIME: 7 ½ TO 10 ½ HOURS

RECOMMENDED WOOD:
OAK OR HICKORY

1 (5- to 7-pound) arm
chuck roast

Vegetable oil, for brushing
the grates

¾ to 1 cup Texas Dry Rub
(page 125)

The arm chuck roast is the cut used to make good old pot roast. While there's nothing wrong with the classic roast, this smoked version takes the cut to a whole new level. The already intense beefy flavor of chuck is magnified by the low and slow smoking process.

**1.** Soak 4½ quarts of wood chips in water for 15 to 30 minutes.

**2.** Bring the roast to room temperature.

**3.** Preheat the smoker to 225°F to 240°F and add the wood chips, following the manufacturer's instructions.

**4.** If the grates haven't been oiled: Roll up a clean, lint-free kitchen towel and dip it into some vegetable oil. Using tongs, grab the towel and rub it across the grates.

**5.** Coat the roast thoroughly in the dry rub and place it on the grates.

**6.** Close the cooking compartment and smoke for 7½ to 10½ hours, or until an instant-read thermometer inserted into the flesh reads 180°F. Soak additional wood chips and replenish as needed; if you no longer see smoke exiting the chimneys or vents, add more wood.

**7.** Let the roast rest for 30 to 45 minutes before serving.

**SMOKING TIP** This recipe assumes a medium pot roast. In general, allow a cooking time of 1½ hours per pound for this cut.

# COFFEE-RUBBED SHORT RIBS

**SERVES 6**

PREP TIME: 30 MINUTES

COOK TIME: 4 TO 5 HOURS

RECOMMENDED WOOD:
OAK OR HICKORY

5 to 6 pounds beef short ribs,
cut into individual ribs

Vegetable oil, for brushing
the grates

1¼ cups Coffee-Chili Dry Rub
(page 120)

While short ribs automatically bring to mind a slow, tender braise, they're also great smoked. It takes time for the fat to render from this rich cut, but the rewards are definitely worthwhile. When they're done smoking, you won't need a fork to cut into them.

**1.** Soak 7½ cups of wood chips in water for 15 to 30 minutes.

**2.** Bring the short ribs to room temperature.

**3.** Preheat the smoker to 200°F to 220°F and add the wood chips, following the manufacturer's instructions.

**4.** If the grates haven't been oiled: Roll up a clean, lint-free kitchen towel and dip it into some vegetable oil. Using tongs, grab the towel and rub it across the grates.

**5.** Coat the ribs thoroughly in the dry rub and place them on the grates.

**6.** Close the cooking compartment and smoke for 4 to 5 hours, or until the ribs are done. Soak additional wood chips and replenish as needed; if you no longer see smoke exiting the chimneys or vents, add more wood.

**7.** Let the ribs rest for 10 minutes, and remove excess fat before serving.

**PAIR IT** A nut brown ale or smoked porter with notes of chocolate and a hint of tang is the perfect beer pairing for these short ribs.

# SMOKED BEEF TENDERLOIN

**SERVES 10**

PREP TIME: 30 MINUTES

COOK TIME: 3 HOURS

RECOMMENDED WOOD: PECAN

1 (4-pound) whole
tenderloin roast

Vegetable oil, for brushing
the grates

½ cup "Good on Everything"
Dry Rub (page 121)

The tenderloin is where the tried-and-true filet mignon comes from. Its claim to fame—incredible tenderness—is also its downfall, at least in the eyes of some chefs, because that means that it is very lean and therefore carries less flavor than fattier cuts. Smoked tenderloin, however, can unite both camps, preserving the cut's tenderness while giving it bold flavor.

1. Soak 4½ cups of wood chips in water for 15 to 30 minutes.

2. Bring the tenderloin to room temperature.

3. Preheat the smoker to 225°F to 240°F and add the wood chips, following the manufacturer's instructions.

4. If the grates haven't been oiled: Roll up a clean, lint-free kitchen towel and dip it into some vegetable oil. Using tongs, grab the towel and rub it across the grates.

5. Coat the tenderloin thoroughly in the dry rub and place it on the grates.

6. Close the cooking compartment and smoke for about 3 hours, or until an instant-read thermometer inserted into the flesh reads 130°F. Soak additional wood chips and replenish as needed; if you no longer see smoke exiting the chimneys or vents, add more wood.

7. Let the tenderloin rest for 10 minutes before serving.

**PAIR IT** Try serving this tenderloin with the elegant Salsa Verde (page 113), which takes just minutes to whip up.

# "ALL DAY LONG" SMOKED BEEF BRISKET

**SERVES 18 TO 24**

PREP TIME: 30 MINUTES

COOK TIME: 10½ TO 13½ HOURS

RECOMMENDED WOOD:
OAK OR HICKORY

1 (7- to 9-pound) packer-trimmed whole beef brisket

Vegetable oil, for brushing the grates

1 cup Texas Dry Rub (page 125)

Down in Texas, this is what barbecue is all about. It's gonna take a while, so make sure you invite some friends over to sit a spell and help watch the smoker.

**1.** Soak 4½ quarts of wood chips in water for 15 to 30 minutes.

**2.** Bring the brisket to room temperature.

**3.** Preheat the smoker to 225°F to 240°F and add the wood chips, following the manufacturer's instructions.

**4.** If the grates haven't been oiled: Roll up a clean, lint-free kitchen towel and dip it into some vegetable oil. Using tongs, grab the towel and rub it across the grates.

**5.** Coat the brisket thoroughly in the dry rub and place it fat-side up on the grates.

**6.** Close the cooking compartment and smoke for 10½ to 13½ hours, or until an instant-read thermometer inserted into the flesh reads at least 195°F. Soak additional wood chips and replenish as needed; if you no longer see smoke exiting the chimneys or vents, add more wood.

**7.** Let the brisket rest for 30 minutes before serving. Slice it thinly against the grain. (If you plan on making Kansas City–Style Burnt Ends, page 79, cut away and reserve the fatty top portion before slicing.)

**PAIR IT** This brisket forms a flavorful bark, or crust, as it cooks, but if you'd like to have a bit of sauce, try the Smoky Texas-Style Barbecue Sauce (page 114).

# FROM THE PITMASTER

**MICHAEL OLLIER**
**CHEF, CERTIFIED ANGUS BEEF**
www.certifiedangusbeef.com

*What tips can you offer for buying and smoking beef brisket?*

The brisket is composed of two parts: the point, which will be the less expensive cut with more fat, and the flat, which is considerably leaner. Both offer great flavor but distinctly different eating experiences.

The brisket is inherently higher in fat than some other beef cuts. Cattle naturally deposit fat in a higher degree toward their front (chuck and brisket areas) and less toward their lower rear (cuts from the round).

The brisket is encased in intermuscular fat (fat between the muscles) and can have generous fat deposits within the lean portion (intramuscular fat). It is this fat, better known as marbling, that is most prized in brisket and is essential considering how brisket is typically cooked: at low temperatures for long times. Marbling keeps the beef tender and juicy and is an essential consideration when choosing beef.

When smoking brisket, I adhere to a classic Texan approach, as best as an Ohio kid can humbly achieve. First, I apply my very own dry rub. Then, I'll smoke with available wood from my region. In the spring, I have access to apple and peach from local orchards, which suits me fine, plus a few logs of hickory along the way. I just avoid the aggressive stuff like mesquite.

In my backyard I use a Weber smoker and am a big fan of it: It makes the process very approachable. I keep the fire building simple, with a blend of natural lump coal and the wood mentioned above.

I smoke in a relatively low environment (215°F) and rely heavily on the thermometer, taking the brisket's internal temperature to 160°F — what's known as the plateau. (That's enough smoke for me!) From there, I employ the "Texas crutch" method: removing the beef from the smoker, wrapping tightly in foil, and then taking it to an internal temperature of 180°F in a preheated 225°F oven.

*Michael Ollier is the corporate chef for the Certified Angus Beef brand.*

# KANSAS CITY–STYLE BURNT ENDS

**SERVES 4 TO 6**

PREP TIME: 30 MINUTES

COOK TIME: 3 TO 4 HOURS

RECOMMENDED WOOD:
OAK OR HICKORY

Fatty top portion from "All Day Long" Smoked Beef Brisket (page 77)

Vegetable oil, for brushing the grates

2 cups "Good on Everything" Dry Rub (page 121)

In Kansas City, they take the fatty top portion of a fully cooked brisket and throw it back in the smoker for some additional love. This might sound like a crazy idea at first—but oh, wait until you pile a few pieces high on slices of white bread and drizzle some Kansas City–Style Barbecue Sauce (page 111) on top. Then you'll see the light.

1. Soak 6 cups of wood chips in water for 15 to 30 minutes.

2. Bring the fatty top portion from the beef brisket to room temperature.

3. Preheat the smoker to 200°F to 220°F and add the wood chips, following the manufacturer's instructions.

4. If the grates haven't been oiled: Roll up a clean, lint-free kitchen towel and dip it into some vegetable oil. Using tongs, grab the towel and rub it across the grates.

5. Coat the fatty top thoroughly in the dry rub and place it on the grates.

6. Close the cooking compartment and smoke for 3 to 4 hours. Soak additional wood chips and replenish as needed; if you no longer see smoke exiting the chimneys or vents, add more wood.

7. Let the burnt end rest for 10 minutes, then slice or shred it before serving.

# CHAPTER SIX

# FISH & SEAFOOD

It may be unusual to think of fish and seafood as part of the barbecue tradition. After all, if a typical barbecue restaurant serves seafood, chances are it's grilled, not smoked. 🦞

But there's plenty of archaeological evidence to indicate that Native Americans were smoking fish over the smoldering remains of fires long before European settlers came to America. Moreover, once upon a time, smoke shacks dedicated to barbecuing fish and seafood dotted the country. Some of those same establishments are still around today, wherever you would expect to find great fish—in the small towns dotting Lake Michigan, the 10,000 lakes of Minnesota, and the cities along the Florida Gulf Coast.

In this chapter, you'll get a taste of how some of these places continue to carry on this tradition.

## TECHNIQUE

Brines are an important first layer of flavor for fish and seafood. Because of their sensitive nature, fish can't spend too much time in brine, so it's important to maximize flavor wherever you can.

In general, fish and seafood are more delicate than their land-based counterparts. There are a few ways you can ensure they remain intact from the moment they come out of the fridge to the moment they come out of the smoker.

Fish fillets and whole fish are transported to and from the smoker using a fish spatula. Fish spatulas differ from regular spatulas in that they are long, slender, and flexible, making it easy to slip them in between the grates and the fish. When placing fish fillets on the grates, make sure to position them skin-side down, which will help them hold together as they smoke. If you wish, you can use a piece of parchment paper or a sheet pan as an extra layer of protection between the skin and the grate.

Shellfish such as shrimp, scallops, and lobster can be handled with your usual long-handled tongs, but maneuver them with care.

To make working with small fish fillets and shellfish easier, invest in a grill rack with a fine mesh, which allows the smoke to circulate along the bottom without letting the food fall through as it cooks.

When it comes to wood, fruitwoods, particularly citrus, work well with fish and seafood. Pecan and grapevines are also good choices. If you're working with salmon, alder and cedar give it incredible flavor.

In general, you'll be smoking fish and seafood at a lower range of temperatures than you would other proteins. Because they cook quickly, lowering the temperature allows more time for the smoke to penetrate thoroughly without overcooking the fish. Most of the recipes in this chapter aim for a temperature of 180°F to 200°F in the cooking compartment.

**Buy wild Alaskan salmon when possible.** It has superior omega-3 content and a better flavor. It is also generally a more sustainable alternative to its farmed counterparts.

**Fillets shouldn't be funky.** When you're buying fish fillets, they should be relatively firm to the touch, smell like fresh fish but not fishy, and feel moist but not wet.

**Whole fish should look fresh.** When buying whole fish, look under the gills to make sure they are bright red. The eyes should be clear, not cloudy.

**Shrimp are sold by count per pound.** So shrimp in the 16-to-20-per-pound range are larger than those in the 21-to-25-per-pound range.

**Look for dry-packed scallops when possible.** Most scallops are frozen and soaked in a phosphate solution that helps preserve them but imparts a soapy flavor.

**Get the best lobster for your buck.** When buying fresh lobster from a tank, look for ones that appear lively and have a thick shell.

**You can't go wrong with a classic.** If you don't want to use the Seafood Dry Rub (page 124), Old Bay Seasoning is a fine substitute.

# BEACH BARBECUE LOBSTER TAILS

**SERVES 4**

PREP TIME: 1 HOUR

COOK TIME: 35 TO 40 MINUTES

RECOMMENDED WOOD:
LEMON OR ORANGE

4 (6- to 7-ounce) lobster tails

4 cups Master Seafood
Marinade (page 132)

Vegetable oil, for brushing
the grates

Lobster is the ultimate summer luxury food. But instead of just boiling or grilling, why not try smoking them? A soy-based seafood marinade gives these tails an Asian flair.

1. In a nonreactive container, submerge the lobster tails in the marinade for 1 hour.

2. Soak 1 cup of wood chips in water for 15 to 30 minutes.

3. Pat the lobster dry.

4. Preheat the smoker to 180°F to 200°F and add the wood chips, following the manufacturer's instructions.

5. If the grates haven't been oiled: Roll up a clean, lint-free kitchen towel and dip it into some vegetable oil. Using tongs, grab the towel and rub it across the grates.

6. Place the lobster tails on the grates.

7. Close the cooking compartment and smoke for 35 to 40 minutes, or until the flesh is opaque.

8. Serve warm or chilled.

**TROUBLESHOOTING** To keep lobster tails from curling up as they cook, insert a butter knife on the underside between the shell and the flesh.

# SMOKED SCALLOPS WITH HERB BUTTER

**SERVES 4**

PREP TIME: 30 MINUTES

COOK TIME: 15 TO 20 MINUTES

RECOMMENDED WOOD: LEMON

Vegetable oil, for brushing
the grates

1 pound sea scallops, halved

1 tablespoon Seafood Dry Rub
(page 124)

½ cup clarified butter or ghee,
at room temperature

2 tablespoons chopped fresh
thyme leaves

Gently smoking scallops accentuates their naturally sweet, briny flavor. With the best-quality scallops, simple herb butter is all you need. When possible, look for dry-packed diver scallops, which have not been soaked in a phosphate solution.

1. Soak 1 cup of wood chips in water for 15 to 30 minutes.

2. Preheat the smoker to 180°F to 200°F and add the wood chips, following the manufacturer's instructions.

3. If the grates haven't been oiled: Roll up a clean, lint-free kitchen towel and dip it into some vegetable oil. Using tongs, grab the towel and rub it across the grates.

4. Season the scallops with the dry rub and place them on a baking sheet on the grates.

5. Close the cooking compartment and smoke for 15 to 20 minutes, or until the scallops are barely opaque.

6. Meanwhile, in a small bowl, stir together the butter and thyme.

7. Serve the scallops immediately with the herb butter.

**PAIR IT** A floral Belgian pale ale would complement the natural sweetness of scallops nicely.

# BARBECUE SHRIMP, REBORN

**SERVES 4**

PREP TIME: 30 MINUTES

COOK TIME: 25 MINUTES

RECOMMENDED WOOD: LEMON

Vegetable oil, for brushing the grates

1 pound large shrimp, peeled and deveined

1 tablespoon Seafood Dry Rub (page 124)

¼ cup unsalted butter, melted

2 tablespoons Worcestershire sauce

1 teaspoon hot sauce

Barbecue shrimp was originally born in New Orleans, where it instantly became a classic. However, the traditional recipe doesn't go anywhere near a smoker—it's sautéed instead—and while it's delicious, it raises the question, what if the shrimp were barbecued? Well, it's time to find out.

1. Soak 1 cup of wood chips in water for 15 to 30 minutes.

2. Preheat the smoker to 180°F to 200°F and add the wood chips, following the manufacturer's instructions.

3. If the grates haven't been oiled: Roll up a clean, lint-free kitchen towel and dip it into some vegetable oil. Using tongs, grab the towel and rub it across the grates.

4. Coat the shrimp thoroughly in the dry rub and place them on the grates in a single layer.

5. Close the cooking compartment and smoke for 25 minutes, or just until the shrimp are opaque.

6. In a bowl, mix together the butter, Worcestershire sauce, and hot sauce; brush on the shrimp.

7. Serve immediately.

**PAIR IT** These shrimp are fantastic with some Sweet 'n' Tangy Green Beans (page 154).

# BARBECUE SHRIMP PO'BOYS

**SERVES 4**

PREP TIME: 5 MINUTES

4 French rolls, split

1 recipe Barbecue Shrimp, Reborn (page 86)

1 cup shredded lettuce

½ cup chopped tomatoes

¼ cup Homemade Mayonnaise (page 110)

Simple, delicious, and tasty, these po'boys are an homage to the classic, which features sautéed shrimp. Pop open a few session lagers, settle into a hammock in the backyard, and enjoy. What more could you want?

**1.** Divide the shrimp among the 4 rolls and top with the lettuce, tomatoes, and mayonnaise.

**2.** Serve immediately.

# SMOKED MAHI MAHI WITH FRESH HERB PASTE

**SERVES 6**

PREP TIME: 2 HOURS

COOK TIME: 2 HOURS

RECOMMENDED WOOD:
LEMON OR ORANGE

2 pounds mahi mahi fillets

8 cups Citrus Brine (page 129)

Vegetable oil, for brushing
the grates

½ cup Fresh Herb Paste
(page 122)

The mild flavor of mahi mahi makes it the perfect canvas for whatever flavors you'd like it to take on. Here, basil and thyme form the basis of an herb paste that keeps the fish from drying out as it cooks.

1. In a nonreactive container, submerge the fish in the brine for 2 hours.

2. Soak 3 cups of wood chips in water for 15 to 30 minutes.

3. Pat the fish dry.

4. Preheat the smoker to 210°F to 225°F and add the wood chips, following the manufacturer's instructions.

5. If the grates haven't been oiled: Roll up a clean, lint-free kitchen towel and dip it into some vegetable oil. Using tongs, grab the towel and rub it across the grates.

6. Coat the fish thoroughly in the herb paste, and place the fillets on parchment paper on top of the grates.

7. Close the cooking compartment and smoke for about 2 hours, or until an instant-read thermometer inserted into the flesh reads at least 145°F. Soak additional wood chips and replenish as needed; if you no longer see smoke exiting the chimneys or vents, add more wood.

8. Let the fish rest for 5 minutes before serving.

**PAIR IT** A citrusy Hefeweizen is a great pairing for these mahi mahi.

# SMOKED WHOLE TROUT

**SERVES 4**

PREP TIME: 30 MINUTES

COOK TIME: 30 TO 45 MINUTES

RECOMMENDED WOOD:
LEMON OR ORANGE

4 (8- to 10-ounce) whole trout,
butterflied

Vegetable oil, for brushing
the grates

2 tablespoons Seafood Dry Rub
(page 124)

Like salmon, trout is a classic choice for barbecued fish. It's rich in fish oil, which keeps it from drying out as it smokes. Here, a simple dry rub forms the main flavor base.

1. Soak 1 cup of wood chips in water for 15 to 30 minutes.

2. Bring the trout to room temperature.

3. Preheat the smoker to 180°F to 200°F and add the wood chips, following the manufacturer's instructions.

4. If the grates haven't been oiled: Roll up a clean, lint-free kitchen towel and dip it into some vegetable oil. Using tongs, grab the towel and rub it across the grates.

5. Coat the trout thoroughly in the dry rub and place them splayed open, skin-side down, on the grates.

6. Close the cooking compartment and smoke for 30 to 45 minutes, or until the flesh flakes easily with a fork.

7. Serve immediately.

**PAIR IT** Swiss Chard with Lemon and Bacon (page 140) has just the right amount of tang to complement the rich flavor of trout.

# MEDITERRANEAN-STYLE SMOKED WHOLE BRANZINO

## SERVES 4 TO 6

PREP TIME: 30 MINUTES

COOK TIME: 20 TO 30 MINUTES

RECOMMENDED WOOD:
LEMON OR ORANGE

4 (1- to 1½-pound) whole branzino

Vegetable oil, for brushing the grates

1 lemon, sliced

10 sprigs fresh oregano

2 tablespoons olive oil

Kosher salt

Branzino, or Mediterranean sea bass, may seem like an unusual choice for barbecued fish, but it has great flavor and stays juicy as it cooks. Here, it's simply coated with olive oil and stuffed with lemon slices and oregano. Serve with Salsa Verde (page 113) if you'd like a sauce.

1. Soak 1 cup of wood chips in water for 15 to 30 minutes.

2. Bring the fish to room temperature.

3. Preheat the smoker to 180°F to 200°F and add the wood chips, following the manufacturer's instructions.

4. If the grates haven't been oiled: Roll up a clean, lint-free kitchen towel and dip it into some vegetable oil. Using tongs, grab the towel and rub it across the grates.

5. Tuck the lemon slices and oregano sprigs among the cavities of the fish, and into several deep cuts in the flesh on each side.

6. Coat the fish thoroughly with the olive oil, season all over with salt, and place on the grates.

7. Close the cooking compartment and smoke for 20 to 30 minutes, or until the flesh flakes easily with a fork.

8. Serve immediately.

**PAIR IT** Looking for the perfect side to go with this fish? Summer Bean Salad (page 153) would be a fine choice.

# CITRUS-SMOKED SALMON FILLET

**SERVES 8**

PREP TIME: 30 MINUTES,
PLUS 2 TO 8 HOURS TO MARINATE

COOK TIME: 1 HOUR

RECOMMENDED WOOD:
ALDER OR CEDAR

1 (3-pound) salmon fillet

3 cups Master Seafood
Marinade (page 132)

Vegetable oil, for brushing
the grates

½ cup Seafood Dry Rub
(page 124)

1 lemon, sliced

½ cup Buttermilk Dressing
(page 109)

Hot-smoked salmon has a distinctive texture. It's firm but flakes easily, which makes it great as a filling for tacos, mixed in with pasta, and yes, stuffed into bagel sandwiches. Keep a careful eye on the temperature to make sure you get great results.

**1.** In a nonreactive container, submerge the salmon in the marinade for 2 to 8 hours.

**2.** Soak 2 cups of wood chips in water for 15 to 30 minutes.

**3.** Pat the salmon dry and let it come to room temperature.

**4.** Preheat the smoker to 180°F to 200°F and add the wood chips, following the manufacturer's instructions.

**5.** If the grates haven't been oiled: Roll up a clean, lint-free kitchen towel and dip it into some vegetable oil. Using tongs, grab the towel and rub it across the grates.

**6.** Coat the salmon thoroughly in the dry rub and place it skin-side down on the grates. Scatter the lemon slices over the flesh.

**7.** Close the cooking compartment and smoke for about 1 hour, or until the flesh flakes easily with a fork. Soak additional wood chips and replenish as needed; if you no longer see smoke exiting the chimneys or vents, add more wood.

**8.** Let the salmon rest for 15 minutes, and serve with the buttermilk dressing.

# BARBECUE FISH TACOS

**SERVES 4**

PREP TIME: 10 MINUTES

1 pound smoked fish, chopped

12 corn tortillas

1 cup Salsa Verde (page 113)

1 cup shredded green cabbage

½ cup chopped cilantro

Cool, crunchy cabbage and zippy salsa verde are the perfect companions to your favorite smoked fish recipe.

**1.** Divide the fish evenly among the tortillas.

**2.** Top with the Salsa Verde, cabbage, and cilantro. Serve immediately.

# FROM THE PITMASTER

**JENNY UNGHBA KORN**
**JUDGE, KANSAS CITY BARBEQUE SOCIETY**
www.kcbs.us

*What's it like to enter a barbecue competition?*

As a barbecue judge certified by the Kansas City Barbeque Society, I am happy to share my experiences of eating and evaluating pounds and pounds of barbecue.

First, for competitors to maximize their chances of winning, they will want to participate in all of the judging categories. For our competition, the categories are chicken, ribs, pork, and brisket. Our judging is blind: The food comes to us in white Styrofoam containers with only a number to differentiate them. We do not know who cooked what, and any attempt to try to convey that information through distinctive decoration within the presentation is prohibited and will likely get an entry disqualified.

In terms of how we judge all the delicious food that goes into our mouths, we have three criteria: taste, appearance, and texture. Because some judges might like barbecue spicy, others may prefer no sauce at all, and still others may wish the brisket had been sliced instead of chopped (both ways are acceptable in our competition), each entry receives an average score across multiple judges, which helps to moderate individual inclinations.

The best advice I have to all serious contenders is to go through the same course I did to become certified as a judge. You don't have to ever use that certification to judge, but the training you receive will provide insight into all the nuances that judges are taught to assess. Visit www.kcbs.us/classes.php to see when and where a certified barbecue judging class is coming to a location near you.

*Jenny Unghba Korn is a lifetime member and judge (#54795) for the Kansas City Barbeque Society.*

# CHAPTER SEVEN

# NOT YOUR EVERYDAY BBQ

Looking for something a little off the beaten path? You've come to the right place. In this chapter, you'll get a taste of what it's like to barbecue some unusual critters.

# TECHNIQUES

Marinades and brines are great with the meats in this chapter, keeping leaner proteins from drying out while adding a layer of flavor. If you wish to tame any gaminess, an overnight soak in buttermilk does wonders.

With leaner meats, it's important to watch the cooking temperatures very carefully to make sure they don't overcook. Buffalo steaks are best rare to medium rare, or at an internal temperature of 125°F to 130°F. Small birds like Cornish game hens and quail should have their legs tied together to keep the body cavity shut as they cook, lest they dry out.

With fattier meats like duck, it's important to render out just the right amount of fat before smoking: Render too little fat and you'll end up chewing on large pieces of it. Render too much and the meat will be dry. The trick is to sear the meat before it goes in the barbecue to release some of the fat between the skin and the flesh; a thin layer about 1/8-inch thick should remain. When you put the meat in the smoker, it's a good idea to place a drip pan underneath the cooking grates, if your smoker allows this, to catch any fat that may drip down. You can use this rendered fat to baste the skin again just before serving for an extra burst of flavor.

**Whatever you're buying, know that the life the animal led has everything to do with the way it tastes.** Was it raised on a balanced diet free of hormones, antibiotics, and other additives? Was it free to roam its natural habitat? If you can answer yes to these questions, then you'll have a better-tasting meal on your plate.

**Take notes.** Whenever you're working with something new or unusual, it's a good idea to keep track of what you're doing so you can look back and see what worked and what didn't.

**Buying lamb? Buy local.** Domestic lamb has a milder flavor than imported lamb because of the way it is raised.

**Buying duck? Buy the right kind.** Muscovy and Peking ducks are the best varieties for smoking.

**Avoid cross-contamination.** Use a separate, nonporous cutting board for prepping raw meat.

# COFFEE-RUBBED BUFFALO STEAK

**SERVES 4**

PREP TIME: 30 MINUTES

COOK TIME: 20 TO 30 MINUTES

RECOMMENDED WOOD: PECAN

**4 (8-ounce) bison steaks**

**Vegetable oil, for brushing the grates**

**2 tablespoons Coffee-Chili Dry Rub (page 120)**

Buffalo, or bison, is a lean and tasty alternative to beef, and it takes surprisingly well to smoking. A coffee-chili dry rub punches up the flavor of the meat, and cooking it to medium rare keeps it nice and juicy.

1. Soak 1 cup of wood chips in water for 15 to 30 minutes.

2. Bring the steaks to room temperature.

3. Preheat the smoker to 200°F to 220°F and add the wood chips, following the manufacturer's instructions.

4. If the grates haven't been oiled: Roll up a clean, lint-free kitchen towel and dip it into some vegetable oil. Using tongs, grab the towel and rub it across the grates.

5. Coat the steaks thoroughly in the dry rub and place them on the grates.

6. Close the cooking compartment and smoke for 20 to 30 minutes, or until an instant-read thermometer inserted into the flesh reads 130°F. Soak additional wood chips and replenish as needed; if you no longer see smoke exiting the chimneys or vents, add more wood.

7. Let the steaks rest for 10 minutes before serving.

# CITRUS-SMOKED CORNISH GAME HEN

PREP TIME: 30 MINUTES,
PLUS 4 HOURS TO MARINATE

COOK TIME: 2 ½ HOURS

RECOMMENDED WOOD: ORANGE

4 Cornish game hens

3 ¼ cups Master Poultry
Marinade (page 131)

Vegetable oil, for brushing
the grates

1 lemon, thinly sliced

⅓ cup "Good on Everything"
Dry Rub (page 121)

⅓ cup Zesty Citrus Sauce
(page 119)

Cornish game hens have delicate flavor that's enhanced by the smoking process. These birds are relatively quick-cooking, and the accompanying citrus sauce is fresh, vibrant, and perfect for summer.

**1.** In a nonreactive container, submerge the hens in the marinade for 4 to 12 hours.

**2.** Soak 3 cups of wood chips in water for 15 to 30 minutes.

**3.** Pat the hens dry and let them come to room temperature.

**4.** Preheat the smoker to 200°F to 220°F and add the wood chips, following the manufacturer's instructions.

**5.** If the grates haven't been oiled: Roll up a clean, lint-free kitchen towel and dip it into some vegetable oil. Using tongs, grab the towel and rub it across the grates.

**6.** Stuff the hens with the lemon, coat them thoroughly in the dry rub, and place them breast-side down on the grates.

**7.** Close the cooking compartment and smoke for 2 ¼ to 2 ½ hours, or until an instant-read thermometer inserted into the flesh without reads 180°F. Soak additional wood chips and replenish as needed; if you no longer see smoke exiting the chimneys or vents, add more wood.

**8.** Let the hens rest for 10 minutes, and serve with the sauce on the side.

**PAIR IT** Sesame-Roasted Asparagus (page 144) is the perfect accompaniment to this delicately flavored bird.

# SMOKED STUFFED QUAIL

**SERVES 4**

PREP TIME: 30 MINUTES

COOK TIME: 1 ½ TO 2 HOURS

RECOMMENDED WOOD:
LEMON OR ORANGE

4 quail

Vegetable oil, for brushing
the grates

10 sprigs fresh thyme

½ lemon, thinly sliced

2 tablespoons Fresh Herb Paste
(page 122)

If you can't get enough of eating tiny little birds but want
something with a more assertive flavor than Cornish
game hens, you may want to try quail. They cook quickly
enough that you can fire these off on a weekday, and their
succulent meat is an interesting change from chicken.

1. Soak 3 cups of wood chips in water for 15 to 30 minutes.

2. Bring the quail to room temperature.

3. Preheat the smoker to 200°F to 220°F and add the wood chips,
following the manufacturer's instructions.

4. If the grates haven't been oiled: Roll up a clean, lint-free kitchen towel
and dip it into some vegetable oil. Using tongs, grab the towel and rub it
across the grates.

5. Stuff the quail with the thyme and lemon, coat them thoroughly in the
herb paste, and tie the legs together to keep the birds from drying out.
Place them breast-side down on the grates.

6. Close the cooking compartment and smoke for 1 ½ to 2 hours, or until
the legs can be pried away easily from the body. Soak additional wood
chips and replenish as needed; if you no longer see smoke exiting the
chimneys or vents, add more wood.

7. Serve immediately.

**PAIR IT** Sure, beer and barbecue go together like pulled pork and
slaw, but for these little birds, a nice citrusy Sauvignon Blanc, Albariño,
or Greco di Tufo would be a nice match, too.

# SMOKED DUCK BREASTS

**SERVES 4**

PREP TIME: 30 MINUTES

COOK TIME: 1 HOUR

RECOMMENDED WOOD:
ORANGE OR PLUM

4 (6-ounce) boneless duck breast halves

Vegetable oil, for brushing the grates

1 tablespoon Coffee-Chili Dry Rub (page 120)

Searing the duck breasts before smoking them renders off some of the fat underneath the skin. It also crisps up the skin nicely. Save the fat for another use, like frying eggs or potatoes.

**1.** Soak 2 cups of wood chips in water for 15 to 30 minutes.

**2.** Pat the duck breasts dry and let them come to room temperature.

**3.** Preheat the smoker to 200°F to 225°F and add the wood chips, following the manufacturer's instructions.

**4.** If the grates haven't been oiled: Roll up a clean, lint-free kitchen towel and dip it into some vegetable oil. Using tongs, grab the towel and rub it across the grates.

**5.** Using a paring knife, make shallow cuts in the skin of the duck breasts without piercing the flesh.

**6.** Heat a large skillet over high heat. When the skillet begins to smoke, add the breasts skin-side down and sear for 5 minutes, or until the skin is crisp and some of the fat has rendered.

**7.** Pour off the fat and reserve it for another use; remove the duck breasts to a cutting board.

**8.** Season the breasts with the dry rub, and place them skin-side up on the grates.

**9.** Close the cooking compartment and smoke for about 1 hour, or until an instant-read thermometer inserted into the flesh reads at least 160°F.

**10.** Let the duck rest for 10 minutes before serving.

**TROUBLESHOOTING** If you can't fit the breasts comfortably in a single pan, sear them in batches.

# SMOKED LAMB CHOPS WITH SALSA VERDE

**SERVES 4**

PREP TIME: 2 HOURS

COOK TIME: 45 TO 55 MINUTES

RECOMMENDED WOOD:
HICKORY OR OAK

8 (5-ounce) lamb loin chops

2 cups Mojo Marinade
(page 133)

Vegetable oil, for brushing
the grates

1 tablespoon Hot 'n' Tangy
Dry Rub (page 123)

1 cup Salsa Verde (page 113)

A quick soak in Mojo Marinade (page 133), a citrus- and garlic-based marinade originating from Cuba, gives these lamb chops a Latin flair. Served with refreshing salsa verde, they're a fantastic summer treat.

1. In a nonreactive container, submerge the lamb chops in the marinade for 2 hours.

2. Soak 2 cups of wood chips in water for 15 to 30 minutes.

3. Pat the lamb chops dry and let them come to room temperature.

4. Preheat the smoker to 200°F to 220°F and add the wood chips, following the manufacturer's instructions.

5. If the grates haven't been oiled: Roll up a clean, lint-free kitchen towel and dip it into some vegetable oil. Using tongs, grab the towel and rub it across the grates.

6. Coat the lamb chops thoroughly in the dry rub and place them on the grates.

7. Close the cooking compartment and smoke for 45 to 55 minutes, or until an instant-read thermometer inserted into the flesh reads at least 140°F.

8. Let the chops rest for 5 minutes and serve with the salsa verde.

# SMOKED FROG LEGS

**SERVES 6 TO 8**

PREP TIME: 30 MINUTES,
PLUS OVERNIGHT TO MARINATE

COOK TIME: 2 HOURS

RECOMMENDED WOOD: ORANGE

3 pounds frog legs

4 cups buttermilk

Vegetable oil, for brushing
the grates

2 tablespoons Seafood Dry Rub
(page 124)

Frog legs, if you've never had them before, taste a bit like a cross between fish and—yes, you guessed it—chicken. They're fun to eat and simply delicious when smoked. An overnight soak in buttermilk neutralizes any strong gamey flavors.

**1.** In a nonreactive container, submerge the frog legs in the buttermilk overnight.

**2.** Soak 3 cups of wood chips in water for 15 to 30 minutes.

**3.** Pat the frog legs dry and let them come to room temperature.

**4.** Preheat the smoker to 225°F to 240°F and add the wood chips, following the manufacturer's instructions.

**5.** If the grates haven't been oiled: Roll up a clean, lint-free kitchen towel and dip it into some vegetable oil. Using tongs, grab the towel and rub it across the grates.

**6.** Coat the frog legs thoroughly in the dry rub and place them on the grates in a single layer.

**7.** Close the cooking compartment and smoke for about 2 hours, or until the flesh separates from the bone easily. Soak additional wood chips and replenish as needed; if you no longer see smoke exiting the chimneys or vents, add more wood.

**8.** Let the frog legs rest for 10 minutes before serving.

**TROUBLESHOOTING** In general, soaking in buttermilk removes off flavors from any game meat.

# SMOKED WHOLE DUCK

**SERVES 4 TO 6**

PREP TIME: 30 MINUTES

COOK TIME: 4 HOURS

RECOMMENDED WOOD:
ORANGE OR PLUM

1 (4-pound) duck

Vegetable oil, for brushing
the grates

⅓ cup Coffee-Chili Dry Rub
(page 120)

If you're a huge fan of dark meat, then a whole smoked duck is definitely worth trying. The bold flavor of the coffee-chili dry rub is an excellent match for the rich duck, and smoking the meat renders it unbelievably juicy and tender.

1. Soak 6 cups of wood chips in water for 15 to 30 minutes.

2. Pat the duck dry and let it come to room temperature.

3. Preheat the smoker to 200°F to 225°F and add the wood chips, following the manufacturer's instructions.

4. If the grates haven't been oiled: Roll up a clean, lint-free kitchen towel and dip it into some vegetable oil. Using tongs, grab the towel and rub it across the grates.

5. Using a paring knife, make shallow cuts in the skin over the breasts without piercing the flesh.

6. Heat a large skillet over high heat. When the skillet begins to smoke, add the duck breast-side down and sear it for 5 minutes, or until the skin is crisp and some of the fat has rendered. Sear the other sides until the skin is crisp all over.

7. Remove the duck to a cutting board. Pour off the fat and reserve it for another use.

8. Season the duck with the dry rub and place it skin-side up on the grates.

9. Close the cooking compartment and smoke for about 4 hours, or until an instant-read thermometer inserted into the flesh without touching the bone reads at least 160°F.

10. Let the duck rest for 10 minutes before serving.

**PAIR IT** A smooth, rich milk stout with a hint of tanginess will pair well with this duck.

CHAPTER EIGHT

# SAUCES, RUBS & MORE

This is the most important chapter in the book. You see, without rubs, sauces, marinades, and brines, barbecue just wouldn't be barbecue. It's pretty rare for a piece of meat, poultry, or seafood to go into a smoker without being dressed in some way. Even in Texas, where they prefer the flavor of the protein to dominate, they'll massage a dry rub into their meat before sending it off to cook.

So, what's the difference between a rub, a marinade, a brine, and a sauce?

**Dry rub.** A dry rub is a combination of dried herbs, spices, salt, and sugar that is applied to the exterior of the protein prior to being cooked. The salt helps bring out the natural flavor of the meat, while the sugar caramelizes a bit during the cooking process.

**Wet rub.** A wet rub is similar to a dry rub, except that it usually incorporates some oil to make it more of a paste. It can also incorporate fresh herbs.

**Marinade.** A marinade is used to impart additional flavors to cuts with a lot of surface area for their weight. They're composed of five things: acid, oil, salt, sugar, and flavoring. The acid can be a fruit juice, vinegar, Worcestershire sauce, beer, wine, or spirits. The oil is usually a neutral vegetable oil that acts as a flavor carrier. The flavoring comes from fresh ingredients like onions, garlic, chiles, and herbs. Marinades intended for lean proteins usually have more oil in them to keep the flesh from being "cooked" by the acid. It's important to marinate in a nonreactive container. In other words, stay away from aluminum, which reacts with acidic foods, and use glass or food-grade plastic instead. As a rule of thumb, 1 cup of marinade is enough to marinate 1 pound of meat.

**Brine.** This is similar to a marinade but simpler. A brine contains salt, water, and a flavoring element. It can also contain sugar. A brine usually has a ratio of water to salt that ranges from 6:1 to 8:1. More salt results in juicier, firmer flesh. Less salt results in more tender flesh that may not be as juicy, so there's a tradeoff. Experiment to see what works best for you. Increasing the amount of time you brine has the same effect as upping the amount of salt in your solution. It's also important to note that this ratio is independent of any other liquids you may add to the brine; so, for example, if you're adding apple juice, it shouldn't factor into your water-to-salt ratio calculation. Brining works through osmosis, resulting in water leaving the protein and concentrating flavor. In exchange, the flavoring element of the brine enters the flesh.

**Sauce.** Most sauces have some sort of base, such as ketchup, tomatoes, mustard, or mayonnaise. They typically have an acidic element, such as vinegar (to thin out the sauce and balance the flavor) as well as a form of sugar. Some sauces can include cooked fresh ingredients, such as onions, garlic, or jalapeños. And just about every sauce incorporates spices and chili powders.

Armed with this knowledge, you'll now have a deeper understanding of how the recipes in this chapter were created and how to start coming up with your own.

# FROM THE PITMASTER

**JORDAN WAKEFIELD**
**CO-OWNER, SMOKE RING**
www.smokeringatlanta.com

***What are your thoughts on marinades, brining, and injections?***

I am a very strong believer in brining most meats. All of my pork and chicken proteins go in a brine for a minimum of 24 hours before hitting the smoke. This mainly helps break down the meat and tenderize the protein. And you can include whatever extra ingredients you want in the brine to add flavor.

I typically use marinades for grilling. Again, these break down proteins, tenderize, and add flavor to the meat.

For my barbecue, I use different dry rubs that I have created to specifically showcase each meat in its own way.

While many people use injections, typically for competitions, in my restaurant we do not use them. Our goal is to encompass the full flavor profile of the meat.

*Jordan Wakefield, together with his wife, owns and operates Smoke Ring, a Georgia-style barbecue house in Atlanta. They are longtime fans of all things Southern and barbecue. Wakefield traces his love of Southern culinary traditions to his father, who was born in Tennessee, a region whose barbecue traditions are recognized around the country. Wakefield is a graduate of Le Cordon Bleu in Atlanta, and his diverse restaurant experience—which includes a stint as lead line cook at Jean-Georges Vongerichten's Spice Market, and later as sous chef and then executive chef at Meehan's Public House in downtown Atlanta—makes him very adept at using Southern food and sensibilities to create cutting-edge cuisine.*

# BUFFALO SAUCE

**MAKES ABOUT 1 CUP**

PREP TIME: 5 MINUTES

COOK TIME: 15 MINUTES

½ cup unsalted butter

6 garlic cloves, finely chopped

½ cup canned diced tomatoes

¼ cup hot sauce, such as Frank's RedHot or Tabasco

1 tablespoon tomato paste

A fresh batch of dry-rubbed, smoked chicken wings is already delicious on its own, but when it's game day, you've got to have Buffalo hot wings. For the ultimate party snack, toss 'em in this fantastic sauce that pays homage to the original from the Anchor Bar in upstate New York. Although tomatoes aren't part of the original recipe, they add a pleasant tang that cuts through the richness of the butter, and it's an addition that Anchor Bar cofounder and sauce inventor Teressa Bellissimo would probably approve.

1. In a small saucepan, melt the butter over medium heat.

2. Add the garlic and cook for 1 to 2 minutes, or until golden.

3. Add the tomatoes and cook for 2 to 3 minutes, or until slightly softened.

4. Add the hot sauce and heat through for 1 to 2 minutes, or until incorporated.

5. Stir in the tomato paste and cook for about 2 minutes, or until incorporated.

6. Let cool, transfer to the bowl of a food processor, and blend thoroughly.

7. Use immediately, or transfer to an airtight container and refrigerate for up to 1 week.

# BUTTERMILK DRESSING

**MAKES ABOUT 1 CUP**

PREP TIME: 5 MINUTES

½ cup Homemade Mayonnaise (page 110), or store-bought

½ cup buttermilk

Juice of ¼ lemon

1 teaspoon kosher salt

1 tablespoon finely chopped fresh dill

Pinch cayenne pepper

Looking for a versatile dressing that you can put together in a snap? Look no further. Buttermilk lends a distinctive tang that contrasts wonderfully with the sweetness of ripe summer tomatoes or the bitterness of crisp lacinato kale. Or, if you want a change of pace from barbecue sauce, you can also serve it on the side with just about any smoked chicken, pork, or game.

**1.** In a medium bowl, whisk together the mayonnaise, buttermilk, lemon juice, salt, dill, and cayenne pepper.

**2.** Use immediately, or transfer to an airtight container and refrigerate for up to 1 week.

# HOMEMADE MAYONNAISE

**MAKES ABOUT 1 CUP**

PREP TIME: 10 MINUTES

1 extra-large egg

1½ cups vegetable oil

Pinch kosher salt

Store-bought mayonnaise is a fine product, but if you're looking for something extraordinary, homemade mayonnaise is worth the effort. If you've never made it before, you'll be surprised at just how simple it really is to make. Once you master the technique, you can get creative and flavor your mayonnaise with just about any fresh herb or spice.

**1.** Place the egg in the bowl of a small food processor. Blend just until the yolk dissolves.

**2.** With the machine running, slowly drizzle in the vegetable oil until the mixture is thickened and resembles mayonnaise.

**3.** Season with the salt.

**4.** Use immediately, or transfer to an airtight container and refrigerate for up to 5 days.

# KANSAS CITY–STYLE BARBECUE SAUCE

**MAKES ABOUT 1 ½ CUPS**

PREP TIME: 10 MINUTES

COOK TIME: 15 MINUTES

### FOR THE SPICE MIXTURE

1 teaspoon black peppercorns

1 teaspoon whole cloves

1 teaspoon cayenne pepper

1 teaspoon ground cinnamon

1 teaspoon kosher salt

1 teaspoon smoked
Spanish paprika

1 teaspoon sweet
Spanish paprika

### FOR THE SAUCE

¼ cup apple cider vinegar

½ cup ketchup

1 tablespoon unsulfured
blackstrap molasses

2 teaspoons
Worcestershire sauce

3 tablespoons light brown sugar

1 tablespoon vegetable oil

3 garlic cloves, finely chopped

½ yellow onion, minced

True to its region's flavors, this sauce is sweet and spicy up front, but cloves balance out the heat at the end with a pleasant vanilla note. This sauce pairs well with pork and chicken.

### TO MAKE THE SPICE MIXTURE

**1.** In a small sauté pan, toast the black peppercorns and cloves over medium heat for 1 to 2 minutes, or until fragrant. Let cool, process thoroughly in a spice grinder, and transfer the mixture to a small bowl.

**2.** To the bowl, add the cayenne pepper, cinnamon, salt, smoked paprika, and sweet paprika. Mix thoroughly and set aside.

### TO MAKE THE SAUCE

**1.** In a medium bowl, whisk together the vinegar, ketchup, molasses, Worcestershire sauce, and sugar to create the wet mixture. Set aside.

**2.** In a medium saucepan, heat the oil over medium heat.

**3.** Add the garlic and onion and cook for 5 to 7 minutes, or until golden.

**4.** Add the ground spice mixture and cook for 10 seconds, or until fragrant.

**5.** Stir in the wet mixture and simmer for about 1 minute, or until the flavors meld.

**6.** Let the sauce cool to room temperature, and refrigerate overnight before using. Keep in an airtight container for up to 3 weeks.

# MILD BARBECUE SAUCE

**MAKES ABOUT 1 CUP**

PREP TIME: 5 MINUTES

COOK TIME: 10 MINUTES

This sauce is a crowd-pleaser: It's well balanced and mild, and it goes well with just about anything. Serve it on the side or slather it on whatever you're smoking in the last 15 minutes of cooking for an extra layer of flavor.

FOR THE SPICE MIXTURE

2 teaspoons cumin seeds

1 tablespoon yellow mustard seeds

1 teaspoon black peppercorns

1 teaspoon white peppercorns

1 teaspoon ground coriander

1 teaspoon kosher salt

1 teaspoon sweet Spanish paprika

1 teaspoon chili powder

FOR THE SAUCE

½ cup distilled white vinegar

½ cup ketchup

1 tablespoon Worcestershire sauce

2 tablespoons unsulfured blackstrap molasses

1 tablespoon vegetable oil

5 garlic cloves, minced

TO MAKE THE SPICE MIXTURE

**1.** In a small sauté pan, toast the cumin seeds, mustard seeds, black peppercorns, and white peppercorns over medium heat for 1 to 2 minutes, or until the mustard seeds start to pop. Let cool, process thoroughly in a spice grinder, and transfer the mixture to a small bowl.

**2.** To the bowl, add the coriander, salt, paprika, and chili powder. Mix thoroughly and set aside.

TO MAKE THE SAUCE

**1.** In a medium bowl, whisk together the vinegar, ketchup, Worcestershire sauce, and molasses to create the wet mixture. Set aside.

**2.** In a medium saucepan, heat the oil over medium heat.

**3.** Add the garlic and cook for about 30 seconds, or until golden.

**4.** Add the spice mixture and cook for 10 seconds, or until fragrant.

**5.** Stir in the wet mixture and simmer for about 1 minute, or until the flavors meld.

**6.** Let the sauce cool to room temperature, and refrigerate overnight before using. Keep in an airtight container for up to 3 weeks.

# SALSA VERDE

**MAKES ABOUT 1 CUP**

PREP TIME: 5 MINUTES

¼ cup extra-virgin olive oil

¼ pound tomatillos, cored and coarsely chopped

1 cup fresh cilantro leaves

1 jalapeño, stemmed, seeded, and coarsely chopped

1 teaspoon kosher salt

1 teaspoon red pepper flakes

2 cups fresh flat-leaf parsley leaves

Juice of ½ lime

In Texas, the barbecue is influenced by the flavors and traditions of Mexico. This fresh, tangy sauce made with tomatillos is fantastic with chicken, beef, or pork. For a flavor boost, try roasting the tomatillos first.

**1.** To the bowl of a small food processor, add the olive oil, tomatillos, cilantro, jalapeño, salt, red pepper flakes, parsley, and lime juice. Blend thoroughly.

**2.** Use immediately, or transfer to an airtight container and refrigerate for up to 5 days.

# SMOKY TEXAS-STYLE BARBECUE SAUCE

**MAKES ABOUT 1 CUP**

PREP TIME: 5 MINUTES

COOK TIME: 15 MINUTES

Toasted cumin and smoked paprika give this barbecue sauce its smokiness, while the chili powders add notes of coffee, fruitiness, and tang, balanced out by the deep flavor of blackstrap molasses.

FOR THE SPICE MIXTURE

1 tablespoon cumin seeds

1 teaspoon black peppercorns

1 tablespoon ancho chili powder

1 tablespoon sweet
Spanish paprika

1 teaspoon cayenne pepper

1 teaspoon chipotle chili powder

1 teaspoon dried oregano,
preferably Mexican

1 teaspoon guajillo chili powder

1 teaspoon kosher salt

7 teaspoons smoked
Spanish paprika

FOR THE SAUCE

1 cup ketchup

½ cup distilled white vinegar

6 tablespoons unsulfured
blackstrap molasses

2 tablespoons vegetable oil

1 jalapeño, stemmed, seeded,
and finely chopped

TO MAKE THE SPICE MIXTURE

**1.** In a small sauté pan, toast the cumin seeds and black peppercorns over medium heat for 1 to 2 minutes, or until fragrant. Let cool, process thoroughly in a spice grinder, and transfer the mixture to a small bowl.

**2.** To the bowl, add the ancho chili powder, sweet paprika, cayenne pepper, chipotle chili powder, oregano, guajillo chili powder, salt, and smoked paprika. Mix thoroughly and set aside.

TO MAKE THE SAUCE

**1.** In a medium bowl, whisk together the ketchup, vinegar, and molasses to create the wet mixture. Set aside.

**2.** In a medium saucepan, heat the oil over medium heat.

**3.** Add the jalapeño and cook for 3 to 4 minutes, or until softened.

**4.** Add the spices and cook for 10 seconds, or until fragrant.

**5.** Stir in the wet mixture and simmer for about 1 minute, or until the flavors meld.

**6.** Let the sauce cool to room temperature, and refrigerate overnight before using. Keep in an airtight container for up to 3 weeks.

# SMOKY TOMATO SAUCE

**MAKES ABOUT 2 CUPS**

PREP TIME: 5 MINUTES

COOK TIME: 25 MINUTES

2 tablespoons extra-virgin olive oil

1 tablespoon cumin seeds

3 garlic cloves, finely chopped

2 cups canned diced tomatoes

Kosher salt

Toasted cumin lends a pleasant smokiness to this tomato sauce, which pairs well with lean cuts of chicken and pork. It's also fantastic with Smoked Meatballs (page 71) in a Knockout Meatball Parm (page 72).

**1.** In a medium saucepan, heat the olive oil over medium heat. Add the cumin and garlic and cook for 5 to 7 minutes, or until the garlic is golden.

**2.** Add the tomatoes and simmer for 10 to 12 minutes, or until the flavors meld. Season with salt.

**3.** Let the sauce cool slightly, then transfer it to the bowl of a food processor; blend thoroughly.

**4.** Use immediately, or transfer to an airtight container. Refrigerate for up to 1 week or freeze for up to 6 months.

# SPICY CAROLINA-STYLE MUSTARD SAUCE

**MAKES ABOUT 1 CUP**

PREP TIME: 5 MINUTES

COOK TIME: 10 MINUTES

¼ cup apple cider vinegar

¼ cup Dijon mustard

¼ cup yellow mustard

1 tablespoon
Worcestershire sauce

3 tablespoons honey

1 tablespoon vegetable oil

1 tablespoon yellow
mustard seeds

1 tablespoon cayenne pepper

1 teaspoon paprika

1 teaspoon kosher salt

In South Carolina, mustard is the base of choice for barbecue sauce, served with all kinds of smoked pork recipes. Pork and mustard, after all, have always been good friends. This version achieves an ideal balance of tanginess, sweetness, and heat, and the use of whole mustard seeds gives the sauce a nice texture.

**1.** In a medium bowl, whisk together the vinegar, Dijon mustard, yellow mustard, Worcestershire sauce, and honey to create the wet mixture. Set aside.

**2.** In a medium saucepan, heat the oil over medium heat.

**3.** Add the mustard seeds and cook for 3 to 5 minutes, or until they start to pop.

**4.** Add the cayenne pepper, paprika, and salt and cook for 10 seconds, or until fragrant.

**5.** Stir in the wet mixture and simmer for about 1 minute, or until the flavors meld.

**6.** Let the sauce cool to room temperature, and refrigerate overnight before using. Keep in an airtight container for up to 3 weeks.

# SPICY CAROLINA-STYLE VINEGAR SAUCE

**MAKES ABOUT 1 ¼ CUPS**

PREP TIME: 1 MINUTE

COOK TIME: 10 MINUTES

2 cups apple cider vinegar

2 tablespoons light brown sugar

1 tablespoon red pepper flakes

2 teaspoons cayenne pepper

1 teaspoon kosher salt

This deceptively simple sauce is absolutely revelatory with pulled pork, the hallmark of Carolina barbecue. In Eastern North Carolina, this is how they do barbecue sauce: no tomato, ketchup, or mustard allowed. Sometimes, the simplest things in life are best.

**1.** In a medium saucepan, stir together the vinegar, sugar, red pepper flakes, cayenne pepper, and salt.

**2.** Bring the mixture to a simmer over medium heat and cook for 3 to 5 minutes, or until the sugar is dissolved.

**3.** Let the sauce cool to room temperature, and refrigerate overnight before using. Keep in an airtight container for up to 1 month.

# "SWEET HOME ALABAMA" BARBECUE SAUCE

**MAKES ABOUT 1 ½ CUPS**

PREP TIME: 5 MINUTES

1 cup Homemade Mayonnaise (page 110), or store-bought

¼ cup apple cider vinegar

1 jalapeño, stemmed, seeded, and finely diced

1 teaspoon kosher salt

1 teaspoon cayenne pepper

If you've never had Alabama white sauce before, the use of mayonnaise as a base may seem a bit unusual. However, this classic sauce is a must-have with any barbecued chicken dish, and one bite will make you a true believer. Just try to save some for everyone else at the table.

**1.** In a small bowl, whisk together the mayonnaise, vinegar, jalapeño, salt, and cayenne pepper.

**2.** Use immediately, or transfer to an airtight container and refrigerate for up to 1 week.

# ZESTY CITRUS SAUCE

**MAKES ABOUT ⅓ CUP**

PREP TIME: 5 MINUTES

COOK TIME: 10 MINUTES

1 tablespoon extra-virgin
olive oil

1 tablespoon all-purpose flour

Juice of ¼ lemon

Juice of 1 mandarin orange

Zest and juice of 1 small
navel orange

1 tablespoon fresh
thyme leaves

This sweet and sour sauce is great with lean chicken and fish dishes. The use of freshly squeezed citrus juice is highly recommended, as it gives the sauce a vibrancy you won't get by using bottled juice. This recipe calls for thyme, but feel free to use whatever herbs you see fit.

**1.** In a small saucepan, heat the olive oil over medium heat.

**2.** Add the flour, and whisk continuously until there are no lumps and the mixture is lightly golden.

**3.** Add the lemon juice, orange juices, orange zest, and thyme.

**4.** Simmer for 1 to 2 minutes, or until slightly thickened.

**5.** Use immediately, or transfer to an airtight container and refrigerate for up to 5 days.

# COFFEE-CHILI DRY RUB

**MAKES ABOUT ¼ CUP**

PREP TIME: 1 MINUTE

1 tablespoon ancho chili powder

1 tablespoon instant coffee

1 tablespoon turbinado sugar

1 teaspoon chipotle chili powder

1 teaspoon guajillo chili powder

2 teaspoons kosher salt

The complex, deep flavors of this dry rub stand up well to rich cuts of beef and pork like brisket and Boston butt. If you happen to have some espresso powder lying around, feel free to use it, but it's worth considering that instant coffee does a fantastic job at a fraction of the cost. The more important thing is to make sure that whatever coffee you use is fresh.

**1.** In a small bowl, stir together the ancho chili powder, instant coffee, sugar, chipotle chili powder, guajillo chili powder, and salt.

**2.** Keep in an airtight container in a cool, dark place for up to 6 months.

# "GOOD ON EVERYTHING" DRY RUB

**MAKES ABOUT ⅓ CUP**

PREP TIME: 1 MINUTE

COOK TIME: 10 MINUTES

1 teaspoon black peppercorns

1 teaspoon coriander seeds

1 teaspoon yellow
mustard seeds

2 teaspoons cumin seeds

1 tablespoon kosher salt

1 tablespoon smoked
Spanish paprika

1 tablespoon sweet
Spanish paprika

1 teaspoon ground cinnamon

2 teaspoons turbinado sugar

No matter what kind of protein you're smoking, applying a dry rub is a great idea. It helps create a wonderful crust—or "bark," if you want to use barbecue lingo, that is a key indicator of good barbecue—especially when it comes to brisket. It also contributes an additional layer of flavor that brings out the essence of your meat, poultry, or fish.

**1.** In a small sauté pan over medium heat, toast the black peppercorns, coriander seeds, mustard seeds, and cumin seeds for 1 to 2 minutes, or until fragrant. Let cool, process thoroughly in a spice grinder, and transfer the mixture to a small bowl.

**2.** To the bowl, add the salt, smoked paprika, sweet paprika, cinnamon, and sugar. Mix thoroughly. Keep in an airtight container in a cool, dark place for up to 1 year.

# FRESH HERB PASTE

**MAKES ABOUT ½ CUP**

PREP TIME: 15 MINUTES

2 cups packed fresh
basil leaves

¼ cup fresh thyme leaves

3 garlic cloves, peeled

1 teaspoon kosher salt

1 teaspoon white peppercorns

1 teaspoon red pepper flakes

¼ cup extra-virgin olive oil

This herb paste, which is a wet rub, works in much the same way as dry rubs. It adds another layer of flavor to the protein you're smoking. This one works best on chicken and seafood; try rubbing it on some salmon or a whole trout before placing it in the cooking chamber of your smoker.

**1.** To the bowl of a small food processor, add the basil, thyme, garlic, salt, peppercorns, red pepper flakes, and olive oil. Process thoroughly.

**2.** Use immediately, or transfer to an airtight container and refrigerate for up to 5 days.

# HOT 'N' TANGY DRY RUB

**MAKES ABOUT ⅓ CUP**

PREP TIME: 1 MINUTE

COOK TIME: 10 MINUTES

2 teaspoons cumin seeds

1 teaspoon black peppercorns

1 teaspoon white peppercorns

1 teaspoon whole cloves

1 tablespoon smoked
Spanish paprika

1 tablespoon sweet
Spanish paprika

1 teaspoon cayenne pepper

1 teaspoon turbinado sugar

2 teaspoons kosher salt

This is the dry rub for those who like their bark to have a little bite. The combination of two different kinds of peppercorns and cayenne creates a lingering, tangy heat that's balanced out by cloves, which have a pleasant sweetness and help put out the fire. Try rubbing this on your favorite cut of chicken, pork, or fish, or better yet, on a beef brisket, for a wickedly hot crust.

**1.** In a small sauté pan over medium heat, toast the cumin seeds, black peppercorns, white peppercorns, and cloves for 1 to 2 minutes, or until fragrant. Let the mixture cool slightly, then process it thoroughly in a spice grinder and transfer it to a small bowl.

**2.** To the bowl, add the smoked paprika, sweet paprika, cayenne pepper, sugar, and salt. Mix thoroughly. Keep in an airtight container in a cool, dark place for up to 1 year.

# SEAFOOD DRY RUB

**MAKES ABOUT ⅓ CUP**

PREP TIME: 1 MINUTE

COOK TIME: 10 MINUTES

1 tablespoon coriander seeds

1 tablespoon yellow mustard seeds

2 teaspoons black peppercorns

2 teaspoons white peppercorns

1 tablespoon sweet Spanish paprika

1 teaspoon dried oregano

1 teaspoon red pepper flakes

1 teaspoon turbinado sugar

2 teaspoons kosher salt

This versatile dry rub is great on just about any type of seafood. Whether you feel like smoking some juicy shrimp, lobster, or even a whole fish, this rub has the right blend of spices to bring out the best in your seafood. If you're a diehard fan of Old Bay Seasoning, feel free to add a bit to the mix.

**1.** In a small sauté pan, toast the coriander seeds, mustard seeds, black peppercorns, and white peppercorns over medium heat for 1 to 2 minutes, or until fragrant. Let the mixture cool slightly, then process it in a spice grinder and transfer it to a small bowl.

**2.** To the bowl, add the paprika, dried oregano, red pepper flakes, sugar, and salt. Mix thoroughly. Keep in an airtight container in a cool, dark place for up to 1 year.

# TEXAS DRY RUB

**MAKES ABOUT ⅓ CUP**

PREP TIME: 1 MINUTE

COOK TIME: 10 MINUTES

1 tablespoon cumin seeds

1 teaspoon black peppercorns

4 teaspoons ancho chili powder

1 tablespoon kosher salt

1 tablespoon smoked
Spanish paprika

1 tablespoon sweet
Spanish paprika

2 teaspoons chipotle
chili powder

1 teaspoon guajillo chili powder

1 teaspoon dried oregano,
preferably Mexican

1 teaspoon turbinado sugar

In Texas, the layering of flavor that comes from coating a nice piece of beef brisket in dry rub is what makes or breaks barbecue. This rub is guaranteed to make your barbecue sing with flavor. In a nod to the neighbors over the border, this dry rub makes generous use of various Mexican chiles in powdered form, which add a smoky complexity.

**1.** In a small sauté pan, toast the cumin seeds and black peppercorns over medium heat for 1 to 2 minutes, or until fragrant. Let the mixture cool slightly, then process it thoroughly in a spice grinder and transfer it to a small bowl.

**2.** To the bowl, add the ancho chili powder, salt, smoked paprika, sweet paprika, chipotle chili powder, guajillo chili powder, oregano, and sugar. Mix thoroughly. Keep in an airtight container in a cool, dark place for up to 1 year.

# ALL-PURPOSE BRINE

**MAKES ABOUT 3 CUPS**

PREP TIME: 1 MINUTE

COOK TIME: 5 MINUTES

2 tablespoons black peppercorns

2 tablespoons white peppercorns

2 tablespoons yellow mustard seeds

3 cups water

½ cup kosher salt

This brine has just five ingredients and is suited to just about any kind of protein you'd like to make juicy and tender. Try using this on chicken, turkey, or lean cuts of pork for best results. You can also tweak the amount of salt in the recipe to tailor it to your needs; less salt results in more tender flesh, while more salt results in firmer, juicier flesh.

**1.** In a medium saucepan, toast the black peppercorns, white peppercorns, and mustard seeds over medium heat for 1 to 2 minutes, or until fragrant.

**2.** Add the water and kosher salt, bring the mixture to a boil to dissolve the salt, and then remove the pan from the heat.

**3.** Let the brine cool to room temperature, then transfer it to an airtight container and refrigerate until completely chilled before using.

# APPLE JUICE BRINE

**MAKES ABOUT 6 CUPS**

PREP TIME: 1 MINUTE

COOK TIME: 5 MINUTES

¼ cup allspice berries

1 tablespoon black peppercorns

1 tablespoon whole cloves

1 tablespoon white peppercorns

3 cups apple juice

3 cups water

½ cup kosher salt

Apple and pork are natural partners, and this brine was created for lean cuts of pork like the loin. Here, the choice of spices brings out the sweetness of apple, but feel free to experiment with other warm spices like cinnamon and nutmeg. If you plan on injecting your brine into your meat, be sure to pass it through a fine-meshed strainer first.

**1.** In a medium saucepan, toast the allspice, black peppercorns, cloves, and white peppercorns over medium heat for 1 to 2 minutes, or until fragrant.

**2.** Add the apple juice, water, and salt, bring the mixture to a boil to dissolve the salt, and then remove the pan from the heat.

**3.** Let the brine cool to room temperature, then transfer it to an airtight container and refrigerate until completely chilled before using.

# BEER MARINADE

**MAKES ABOUT 2 CUPS**

PREP TIME: 1 MINUTE

COOK TIME: 5 MINUTES

¼ cup extra-virgin olive oil

1 tablespoon dried oregano

1 tablespoon yellow
mustard seeds

2 tablespoons coriander seeds

2 cups American lager, such as
Budweiser

1 tablespoon kosher salt

1 tablespoon light brown sugar

There are few things in life that beer doesn't improve, and marinade is no exception. This mildly flavored marinade does wonders on chicken and pork. Try experimenting with different brands and styles of beer to find your favorite flavor profile.

**1.** In a medium saucepan, heat the oil over medium heat. Add the oregano, mustard seeds, and coriander seeds and cook for 1 to 2 minutes, or until fragrant.

**2.** Turn off the heat and add the beer, salt, and sugar. Whisk to dissolve.

**3.** Let the marinade cool to room temperature, transfer it to an airtight container, and refrigerate until completely chilled before using.

# CITRUS BRINE

**MAKES ABOUT 4 CUPS**

PREP TIME: 1 MINUTE

COOK TIME: 5 MINUTES

¼ cup yellow mustard seeds

2 tablespoons coriander seeds

2 tablespoons white peppercorns

2 cups orange juice

2 cups water

¼ cup kosher salt

This simple citrus-flavored brine is a perfect match for lean cuts of poultry as well as all kinds of seafood. The delicate lime flavor of coriander seeds and the savory white peppercorns really come alive when toasted.

**1.** In a medium saucepan, toast the mustard seeds, coriander seeds, and white peppercorns over medium heat for 1 to 2 minutes, or until fragrant.

**2.** Add the orange juice, water, and salt, bring the mixture to a boil to dissolve the salt, and then remove the pan from the heat.

**3.** Let the brine cool to room temperature, then transfer it to an airtight container and refrigerate until completely chilled before using.

# MASTER PORK MARINADE

**MAKES ABOUT 2 CUPS**

PREP TIME: 1 MINUTE

COOK TIME: 10 MINUTES

3 tablespoons extra-virgin
olive oil

2 tablespoons allspice berries

1 tablespoon black peppercorns

1 tablespoon white peppercorns

1 teaspoon whole cloves

2 cups beef broth

1 tablespoon honey

1 tablespoon kosher salt

1 tablespoon unsulfured
blackstrap molasses

2 tablespoons apple
cider vinegar

The combination of toasted warm spices, honey, and blackstrap molasses will give pork a subtle sweetness and complexity of flavor that is simply sublime when balanced out by a touch of apple cider vinegar. Use this marinade to liven up lean cuts of pork like the loin. You can soak smaller cuts for a few hours and larger cuts overnight.

**1.** In a medium saucepan, heat the oil over medium heat. Add the allspice berries, black peppercorns, white peppercorns, and cloves, and cook for 1 to 2 minutes, or until fragrant.

**2.** Add the beef broth, honey, salt, and molasses. Bring the mixture to a boil to dissolve the salt, then remove the pan from the heat.

**3.** Let the marinade cool to room temperature and stir in the apple cider vinegar.

**4.** Transfer to an airtight container, and refrigerate until completely chilled before using.

# MASTER POULTRY MARINADE

**MAKES ABOUT 2 CUPS**

PREP TIME: 1 MINUTE

COOK TIME: 10 MINUTES

¼ cup extra-virgin olive oil

1 tablespoon black peppercorns

1 tablespoon white peppercorns

1 teaspoon whole cloves

5 garlic cloves, crushed

2 cups chicken broth

1 tablespoon cane sugar

1 tablespoon kosher salt

20 sprigs fresh thyme

Juice of 1 lemon

The combination of herbs and spices in this marinade complements the natural flavor of chicken, turkey, and other types of poultry. Give your chicken breasts a flavor boost before tossing them in a smoker with this marinade, or if you're feeling ambitious, make a large batch and marinate a whole bird. The sky's the limit!

**1.** In a medium saucepan, heat the oil over medium heat. Add the black peppercorns, white peppercorns, cloves, and garlic and cook for 1 to 2 minutes, or until fragrant.

**2.** Add the chicken broth, sugar, salt, and thyme. Bring the mixture to a boil to dissolve the sugar and salt, then remove the pan from the heat.

**3.** Let the marinade cool to room temperature and stir in the lemon juice.

**4.** Transfer to an airtight container, and refrigerate until completely chilled before using.

# MASTER SEAFOOD MARINADE

**MAKES ABOUT 2 CUPS**

PREP TIME: 1 MINUTE

COOK TIME: 10 MINUTES

¼ cup extra-virgin olive oil

2 tablespoons coriander seeds

1 tablespoon dried oregano

1 tablespoon white peppercorns

1 tablespoon yellow
mustard seeds

½ cup soy sauce

1 tablespoon cane sugar

1½ cups water

Juice of ½ lemon

This marinade takes things in a slightly different direction by incorporating a burst of savory flavor from soy sauce, which pairs nicely with oregano and white peppercorns. This marinade works well on whole fish, fish fillets, shrimp, lobster—just about any type of seafood.

**1.** In a medium saucepan, heat the oil over medium heat. Add the coriander, oregano, peppercorns, and mustard seeds and cook for 1 to 2 minutes, or until fragrant.

**2.** Add the soy sauce, sugar, and water. Bring the mixture to a boil to dissolve the sugar, then remove the pan from the heat.

**3.** Let the marinade cool to room temperature, then stir in the lemon juice.

**4.** Transfer to an airtight container, and refrigerate until completely chilled before using.

# MOJO MARINADE

**MAKES ABOUT 2 CUPS**

PREP TIME: 1 MINUTE

COOK TIME: 10 MINUTES

1 cup extra-virgin olive oil

10 garlic cloves, smashed

1 tablespoon dried oregano

½ cup orange juice

Juice of ½ lemon

Juice of 1½ limes

1 tablespoon kosher salt

Stems of 1 bunch cilantro

Mojo marinade originated in Cuba, where it's used to marinate large cuts of pork. However, its bright, citrusy flavors work equally well on chicken or fish. The generous amount of olive oil keeps the flesh from getting "cooked" by all the acid in the citrus while allowing the flavors to permeate.

**1.** In a medium saucepan, heat the oil over medium heat. Add the garlic and oregano and cook for 1 to 2 minutes, or until fragrant.

**2.** Turn off the heat and let the garlic-oregano mixture cool slightly, then stir in the orange juice, lemon juice, lime juice, salt, and cilantro stems.

**3.** Transfer to an airtight container, and refrigerate until completely chilled before using.

# CHAPTER NINE

# AMAZING BBQ SIDES

No barbecue would be complete without some great sides to accompany the main event. Whether you're smoking a whole brisket, pork shoulder, or even just a few chicken breasts or some barbecued shrimp, it just wouldn't be the same without all the fixin's.

There's definitely some room for creativity when pairing side dishes with smoked meats, poultry, and seafood, but here are some good pairings to keep in mind.

Did you spend all day hard at work on smoking a Boston butt? Well then, naturally you've got to have some Simple Cole Slaw (page 138) to go with that pulled pork. Or perhaps you smoked a whole trout? You'll want some simple Sesame-Roasted Asparagus (page 144) with it. And no matter what you made, Classic Potato Salad (page 151), Easy Macaroni Salad (page 152), and Wild West Baked Beans (page 156) should be part of any spread.

Does this sound exciting? It should! Just like with Thanksgiving dinner, the sides at a barbecue should be just as exciting as the centerpiece on the table.

## BEER AND WHISKEY PAIRINGS

A barbecue wouldn't be complete without some great beer. But if you really want the flavors of your barbecue to shine, you've got to think beyond the usual six-pack and look at all the different styles available to match with what you're cooking. Here's a basic guide.

◈ **Lean poultry and pork loin.** Saison or farmhouse ale, such as Ommegang Brewery's Hennepin or Goose Island's Sofie

◈ **Pork ribs.** German-style schwarzbiers, such as Samuel Adams Black Lager or Köstritzer Schwarzbier

◈ **Pork shoulder.** Amber ale or lager, such as Fat Tire Amber Ale or Blue Point Toasted Lager

◈ **Beef brisket and duck.** Oktoberfest-style amber, such as Spaten Oktoberfestbier or Paulaner Oktoberfest

◈ **Beef tenderloin and buffalo.** Full-bodied Belgian ale such as Ommegang Abbey Ale or Chimay Red

◈ **Seafood.** Wheat beers such as Lagunitas A Little Sumpin' Sumpin' or Anchor Summer Beer

Barrel-aged whiskey—in particular, bourbon—is also a great match for smoked meats. In the barrel, whiskey's natural sweetness is augmented by hints of smokiness, vanilla, and other flavors and aromas that complement barbecue nicely. Look for mid-range bottles ($30 and under) that don't have too much alcohol and offer balanced flavor that won't overwhelm your food. Elijah Craig's Kentucky Bourbon 12 Years Old, Buffalo Trace, and Bulleit Bourbon are good ones to try.

# HEIRLOOM TOMATO SALAD WITH BUTTERMILK DRESSING

**SERVES 4**

PREP TIME: 10 MINUTES

1 pound heirloom tomatoes, cored and cut into ½-inch-thick slices

¼ cup Buttermilk Dressing (page 109)

½ cup torn fresh basil leaves

Kosher salt

Freshly ground black pepper

Tomatoes are just one of those things that shouldn't be eaten out of season—not raw, at least. So when summer is in full swing and the farmers' market is alive with color, take full advantage of the bounty, get some great tomatoes, and make this salad. You'll be glad you did.

**1.** Lay the tomatoes out on a serving platter, drizzle them with the dressing, and top with the basil.

**2.** Season with salt and pepper and serve immediately.

# SIMPLE COLE SLAW

**SERVES 4**

PREP TIME: 15 MINUTES

No barbecue would be complete without a little slaw on the side. This is especially good with pulled pork. Just pile them together on some buns and drizzle a little barbecue sauce on top, and you've got one heck of a sandwich.

## FOR THE DRESSING

1 tablespoon cane sugar

2 teaspoons kosher salt

1 tablespoon apple cider vinegar

¼ cup Homemade Mayonnaise (page 110), or store-bought

## FOR THE SALAD

3 carrots, shredded

¼ head red cabbage, cored and thinly sliced

¼ head green cabbage, cored and thinly sliced

2 radishes, thinly sliced

### TO MAKE THE DRESSING

**1.** In a large bowl, whisk together the sugar, salt, and vinegar until the sugar and salt are fully dissolved.

**2.** Add the mayonnaise, and whisk until incorporated.

### TO MAKE THE SALAD

**1.** To the bowl with the dressing, add the carrots, red cabbage, green cabbage, and radishes.

**2.** Toss until well coated and refrigerate for 30 minutes before serving.

# GARLICKY SAUTÉED SPINACH

**SERVES 4**

PREP TIME: 10 MINUTES

COOK TIME: 15 MINUTES

1 tablespoon extra-virgin olive oil

½ yellow onion, finely diced

5 garlic cloves, thinly sliced

1½ pounds spinach

¼ cup chicken broth

Kosher salt

When you've got great spinach, there isn't a whole lot you have to do to it. Forget about the stuff that comes in the 5-ounce plastic bags. If spinach is in season (yeah, it's a winter green), spring for the best at the farmers' market.

1. In a large sauté pan, heat the olive oil over medium heat.

2. Add the onion and garlic and cook for 5 to 7 minutes, or until golden.

3. Add the spinach and chicken broth and cook for 5 to 7 minutes, or until the spinach is wilted.

4. Season with salt, divide among 4 plates, and serve immediately.

# SWISS CHARD WITH LEMON AND BACON

**SERVES 4**

PREP TIME: 10 MINUTES

COOK TIME: 20 MINUTES

4 strips bacon

2 pounds Swiss chard, stems finely chopped, leaves chopped

Kosher salt

Juice of ½ lemon

The flavor of Swiss chard is pretty close to spinach, but it's a little heartier in composition and can stand up nicely to savory preparations. That's why this recipe pairs it with bacon and lemon, which add both richness and tang.

**1.** In a large sauté pan, cook the bacon over high heat for 1½ to 2 minutes, or until crisp on one side.

**2.** Reduce the heat to medium, flip the bacon, and cook the other side for 1 to 2 minutes.

**3.** Remove the bacon from the pan and set it aside.

**4.** Add the chard stems and cook for 7 to 9 minutes, or until softened.

**5.** Add the chard leaves and cook for 1 to 2 minutes, or until just wilted. Season with salt.

**6.** Turn off the heat, let the chard cool for 1 minute, and stir in the lemon juice.

**7.** Crumble the bacon over top, divide the chard mixture among 4 plates, and serve immediately.

# TRIED-AND-TRUE KALE SALAD

**SERVES 4**

PREP TIME: 20 MINUTES

2 pounds lacinato kale, center stems removed and discarded

½ cup Buttermilk Dressing (page 109)

Kosher salt

Freshly ground black pepper

When it comes to making good kale salad, it's all about technique, beginning with the type of kale you choose. The best kale for salad is lacinato kale, which has thin, long leaves that tenderize nicely. Speaking of tenderizing, think of kale as the opposite of every salad green you've ever worked with: It actually benefits from some tough love. So get in there, and don't be afraid to take out your frustrations on it.

**1.** Do this in two batches: Crumple up the kale and massage it vigorously with your hands to tenderize.

**2.** Pour the dressing into the bottom of a large bowl, toss in the kale, and coat the kale with the dressing using your hands.

**3.** Season with salt and pepper, divide among 4 plates, and serve immediately.

# SAUTÉED KALE AND ONIONS

**SERVES 4**

PREP TIME: 10 MINUTES

COOK TIME: 20 MINUTES

2 tablespoons extra-virgin olive oil

2 yellow onions, chopped

10 garlic cloves, chopped

2 pounds lacinato kale, center stems removed and discarded, leaves chopped

½ cup chicken broth

Kosher salt

Freshly ground black pepper

Love kale, but don't feel like having a salad? Sautéing kale turns it nice and tender while also tempering its natural bitterness. For a twist, try using shallots instead of onions.

**1.** In a large sauté pan, heat the olive oil over medium-high heat.

**2.** Add the onions and garlic and cook for 7 to 9 minutes, or until golden brown.

**3.** Add the kale and chicken broth, and season with salt and pepper.

**4.** Cook, stirring occasionally, for 5 to 7 minutes, or until the kale is tender.

**5.** Divide the kale among 4 plates and serve immediately.

# SOUTHERN-STYLE COLLARD GREENS

**SERVES 4**

PREP TIME: 10 MINUTES

COOK TIME: 35 MINUTES

3 strips bacon

1 pound collard greens,
coarsely chopped

¾ cup chicken broth

1 cup diced canned tomatoes

2 tablespoons distilled
white vinegar

2 tablespoons light brown sugar

Kosher salt

Freshly ground black pepper

These collard greens are just like Grandma used to make 'em. Well, someone's grandma, at least. Point is, they're just delicious.

**1.** In a large pot with a lid, cook the bacon over high heat for 1½ to 2 minutes, or until crisp on one side.

**2.** Reduce the heat to medium, flip the bacon, and cook the other side for 1 to 2 minutes.

**3.** Remove the bacon from the pot and set it aside.

**4.** Add the collard greens, chicken broth, tomatoes, vinegar, and sugar to the pot, and season with salt and pepper.

**5.** Cover the pot, reduce the heat to medium-low, and cool for 30 minutes, or until the collards are tender.

**6.** Crumble the bacon over top, divide the collards among 4 plates, and serve immediately.

# SESAME-ROASTED ASPARAGUS

**SERVES 4**

PREP TIME: 5 MINUTES

COOK TIME: 25 TO 35 MINUTES

2 pounds asparagus, woody ends trimmed

1 tablespoon extra-virgin olive oil

1 tablespoon vegetable oil

4 teaspoons sesame seeds

Kosher salt

Asparagus is another one of those seasonal treats that doesn't need a complicated preparation to make it shine. This is especially true if you have the first asparagus of the season; thin tendrils of sweetness announce the arrival of spring just the same as the return of geese from the south. Pair this side with lean chicken or delicate fish dishes.

1. Preheat the oven to 450°F.

2. In a baking dish or oven-safe skillet, arrange the asparagus in a single layer, and coat with the olive oil, vegetable oil, and sesame seeds. Season with salt.

3. Roast in the oven for 15 to 25 minutes, depending on the thickness of the spears, until tender.

4. Divide the asparagus among 4 plates and serve immediately.

# RADISH AND BEET SALAD WITH BASIL

**SERVES 4**

PREP TIME: 10 MINUTES

COOK TIME: 40 TO 55 MINUTES

12 baby beets, trimmed

Juice of ½ lemon

2 tablespoons extra-virgin olive oil

1 teaspoon kosher salt, plus more for the boiling water

Freshly ground black pepper

4 radishes, cut into ¼-inch dice

½ cup thinly sliced fresh basil

This cool and crunchy salad is just what you need to refresh your palate between bites of succulent pulled pork, smoky brisket, or juicy beer can chicken. The spicy and cool radishes contrast wonderfully with the sweet, toothsome beets, and the peppery sweetness of basil rounds out the flavors at the end of each bite. Who knew a salad without greens could be so exciting?

**1.** In a medium pot, cover the beets with cold water by 1 inch, salt the water until it tastes like the sea, and bring it to a boil over high heat. Fill a large bowl with ice water and set it nearby.

**2.** Boil the beets for 25 to 40 minutes, depending on their size, or until fork tender.

**3.** Remove the pot from the heat, and, using tongs or a slotted spoon, transfer the beets to the ice water. When they are cool enough to handle, drain the beets, brush off their skins, and cut them into ¼-inch dice.

**4.** In a large bowl, whisk together the lemon juice, olive oil, 1 teaspoon salt, and pepper.

**5.** Add the beets, radishes, and basil, and toss until well coated.

**6.** Divide the salad among 4 plates and serve immediately.

# GRILLED CORN ON THE COB WITH HERB BUTTER

**SERVES 4**

PREP TIME: 5 MINUTES

COOK TIME: 20 MINUTES

2 tablespoons chopped
fresh thyme

½ cup clarified butter or ghee,
at room temperature

4 ears corn, husked

Kosher salt

Freshly ground black pepper

Summer just wouldn't be the same without corn on the cob. Grilling corn brings out its natural sweetness, and a little herb butter complements that sweetness nicely.

1. Preheat a grill on medium-high heat.

2. In a small bowl, stir the thyme into the butter.

3. Brush the corn generously with the herb butter, and season with salt and pepper.

4. Grill the corn, turning occasionally, for 7 to 9 minutes, or until slightly charred in spots.

5. Serve immediately with the remaining herb butter on the side.

# FOIL-WRAPPED MUSHROOMS WITH FRESH HERBS

**SERVES 4**

PREP TIME: 5 MINUTES

COOK TIME: 1 HOUR

1 pound mixed mushrooms

6 tablespoons extra-virgin olive oil

10 to 20 sprigs mixed fresh hardy herbs, such as rosemary or thyme

½ cup red or white wine

Kosher salt

If you're already in front of the smoker all day and you've got some spare real estate on the grate, you might as well cook a side dish in there, right? Right. This one's real easy.

**1.** Divide the mushrooms, olive oil, herbs, and wine evenly between two pieces of aluminum foil, season with salt, and wrap them tightly.

**2.** Place the foil packets in the smoker at 250°F for 60 minutes, or until cooked through.

**3.** Divide the mushrooms among 4 plates and serve immediately.

# ROASTED CAULIFLOWER WITH HONEY-SOY GLAZE

**SERVES 4**

PREP TIME: 5 MINUTES

COOK TIME: 35 MINUTES

¼ cup honey

2 tablespoons soy sauce

1 head cauliflower,
cut into florets

4 teaspoons sesame seeds

Nutty cauliflower gets a burst of Asian flavor with a simple honey-soy glaze. This is a great side dish that pairs well with chicken and pork.

**1.** Preheat the oven to 450°F.

**2.** In a small bowl, mix together the honey and soy sauce to make the glaze.

**3.** Place the cauliflower in a large, oven-safe skillet, add in the glaze and sesame seeds, and toss well to combine.

**4.** Transfer the skillet to the oven and roast for 20 to 25 minutes, or until the cauliflower is tender.

**5.** Remove the skillet from the oven and place it on the stove over high heat.

**6.** Bring the glaze to a boil, tossing the cauliflower frequently until it is well coated and most of the glaze has evaporated.

**7.** Divide the cauliflower among 4 plates and serve immediately.

# ORANGE ZEST SUNCHOKES

**SERVES 4**

PREP TIME: 10 MINUTES

COOK TIME: 45 MINUTES

1 ⅓ pounds sunchokes

Kosher salt

2 tablespoons extra-virgin olive oil

2 tablespoons vegetable oil

Zest of 1 orange

¼ cup thinly sliced fresh basil

Sunchokes, or Jerusalem artichokes, are simply wonderful. Their season generally lasts from fall through spring, and they look a bit like knobs of ginger. Their flavor can be described as a cross between celery and waxy potatoes, and they're fantastic roasted.

**1.** Preheat the oven to 450°F.

**2.** In a medium pot, cover the sunchokes with cold water by 1 inch, salt the water until it tastes like the sea, and bring it to a boil over high heat.

**3.** Cook the sunchokes for 15 to 17 minutes, or until they are nearly fork tender.

**4.** Meanwhile, heat the olive oil and vegetable oil in a large, oven-safe skillet over medium heat. Add the orange zest and cook for 4 to 5 minutes or until fragrant.

**5.** Turn off the heat and set the skillet aside for about 10 minutes to allow the flavors to infuse.

**6.** Drain the sunchokes, add them to the skillet, and stir to coat them with the oil.

**7.** Transfer the skillet to the top rack of the oven and roast for 20 to 25 minutes, or until the sunchokes are fork tender.

**8.** Top with the basil just before serving, and divide among 4 plates.

# DIJON POTATO SALAD

**SERVES 4**

PREP TIME: 5 MINUTES

COOK TIME: 35 MINUTES

This potato salad borrows a bit of inspiration from our Gaelic neighbors across the pond. Dijon mustard lends some kick to a dressing that mellows out with the addition of some fresh herbs—in this case, dill and parsley, which are excellent partners for fingerling potatoes.

### FOR THE DRESSING

2 tablespoons Dijon mustard

Juice of ½ lemon

½ teaspoon kosher salt

6 tablespoons extra-virgin olive oil

### FOR THE SALAD

1 ¼ pounds fingerling potatoes

Kosher salt

1 tablespoon finely chopped fresh dill

1 tablespoon finely chopped fresh flat-leaf parsley

### TO MAKE THE DRESSING

In a medium bowl, whisk together the mustard, lemon juice, salt, and olive oil. Set aside.

### TO MAKE THE SALAD

1. In a medium pot, cover the potatoes with cold water by 1 inch, salt the water until it tastes like the sea, and bring it to a boil over high heat.

2. Boil the potatoes for 13 to 15 minutes, or until fork tender.

3. Drain the potatoes, let them cool slightly, and then cut them into ¼-inch-thick slices. Transfer the potatoes to the bowl with the dressing.

4. Add the dill and parsley, and toss until well coated.

5. Divide the salad among 4 plates and serve immediately.

# CLASSIC POTATO SALAD

**SERVES 4**

PREP TIME: 5 MINUTES

COOK TIME: 35 MINUTES

### FOR THE DRESSING

⅓ cup Homemade Mayonnaise (page 110), or store-bought

4 teaspoons apple cider vinegar

½ teaspoon kosher salt

### FOR THE SALAD

1¼ pounds baby red and white potatoes

Kosher salt

3 celery stalks

2 scallions, green and white parts thinly sliced

Simplicity is the secret to many classic dishes, and this potato salad is no exception. Perfectly cooked baby potatoes are coated in a rich, mayonnaise-based dressing with just a touch of vinegar and tossed with celery and scallions for a bit of crunch and allium flavor.

### TO MAKE THE DRESSING

In a medium bowl, whisk together the mayonnaise, vinegar, and salt. Set aside.

### TO MAKE THE SALAD

**1.** In a medium pot, cover the potatoes with cold water by 1 inch, salt the water until it tastes like the sea, and bring it to a boil over high heat.

**2.** Boil the potatoes for 13 to 15 minutes, or until fork tender.

**3.** Drain the potatoes, let them cool slightly, and cut them into halves or quarters, depending on their size. Transfer to the bowl with the dressing.

**4.** Finely chop the celery stalks and their leaves, if they look fresh. Add them to the bowl together with the scallions, and toss until well coated.

**5.** Divide the salad among 4 plates and serve immediately.

# EASY MACARONI SALAD

**SERVES 4**

PREP TIME: 10 MINUTES

COOK TIME: 15 MINUTES

Kosher salt

1½ cups dried macaroni

½ cup Homemade Mayonnaise
(page 110), or store-bought

Juice of ¼ lemon

3 celery stalks, finely chopped,
including leaves if they
are fresh

1 red bell pepper, finely chopped

Freshly ground black pepper

Need a classic barbecue side dish that you can put together in just about no time? Yeah, who doesn't, especially after a 12-hour smoke job like a brisket. This classic macaroni salad is just the ticket.

**1.** Fill a medium pot with water, salt it until it tastes like the sea, and bring it to a boil over high heat.

**2.** Add the macaroni and cook for 5 minutes, or until al dente, then remove the pot from the heat. Drain the pasta in a colander and run it under cold water until it comes to room temperature.

**3.** In a medium bowl, whisk together the mayonnaise and lemon juice.

**4.** Add the macaroni, celery, and bell pepper, and toss until well coated.

**5.** Season with salt and pepper, divide the salad among 4 plates, and serve immediately.

# SUMMER BEAN SALAD

**SERVES 4**

PREP TIME: 15 MINUTES

COOK TIME: 10 MINUTES

Kosher salt

¾ pound green and yellow wax beans, trimmed

2 cups mixed cherry tomatoes, halved

¼ cup Buttermilk Dressing (page 109)

½ cup torn fresh basil leaves

Freshly ground black pepper

This simple salad showcases the natural goodness of fresh summer beans and cherry tomatoes. The buttermilk dressing serves as a pleasant, tangy counterpoint to their sweetness.

**1.** Fill a medium pot with water, salt it until it tastes like the sea, and bring it to a boil over high heat. Fill a large bowl with ice water and set it nearby.

**2.** Add the beans to the boiling water and cook for 4 to 5 minutes, or until crisp-tender.

**3.** Remove the pot from the heat and use a slotted spoon to transfer the beans to the bowl of ice water. Let them cool for a few minutes, then drain them well.

**4.** Pat the beans dry, and chop them into bite-size pieces.

**5.** In a large bowl, toss together the beans, tomatoes, and dressing until well coated. Top with the basil, and season with salt and pepper.

**6.** Divide the salad among 4 plates and serve immediately.

# SWEET 'N' TANGY GREEN BEANS

**SERVES 4**

PREP TIME: 10 MINUTES

COOK TIME: 60 MINUTES

1 tablespoon extra-virgin olive oil

1 yellow onion, finely diced

1 pound green beans, trimmed

2 cups canned diced tomatoes

1½ cups chicken broth

¼ cup distilled white vinegar

¼ cup light brown sugar

It's true: Go to any good steam-table restaurant in the South that serves green beans, and you'll find they're absolutely delicious, if a little on the soft side. This version maintains the delicate balance of sweet and tangy while allowing the beans to retain some snap.

1. In a large sauté pan, heat the olive oil over medium heat.

2. Add the onion and cook for 5 to 7 minutes, or until softened.

3. Add the beans, tomatoes, chicken broth, vinegar, and sugar.

4. Bring the mixture to a simmer and cook the beans for 40 to 50 minutes, or until crisp-tender.

5. Divide the beans among 4 plates and serve immediately.

# BUTTERY MASHED POTATOES

**SERVES 4**

PREP TIME: 5 MINUTES

COOK TIME: 45 MINUTES

1¼ pounds red potatoes

Kosher salt

1 cup whole milk, warmed

½ cup unsalted butter, cold

1 teaspoon freshly ground
black pepper

¼ cup finely chopped mixed
fresh herbs, such as dill,
tarragon, thyme, or parsley

Sometimes, you just really want some good mashed potatoes. Well, look no further. These mashed potatoes are simply delicious.

**1.** Place the potatoes in a medium pot and cover them with cold water by 1 inch. Salt the water until it tastes like the sea, and bring it to a boil over high heat.

**2.** Boil the potatoes for 25 to 30 minutes, or until fork tender.

**3.** Remove the pot from the heat. Drain the potatoes, let them cool slightly, and then transfer them to a medium bowl.

**4.** Add the milk and butter, and mash until smooth.

**5.** Season with salt, add the pepper, and stir in the fresh herbs.

# WILD WEST BAKED BEANS

**SERVES 8**

PREP TIME: 5 MINUTES PLUS
OVERNIGHT SOAKING

COOK TIME: 2 HOURS

2½ cups dried navy beans

7½ cups water

3 strips bacon

1 tablespoon tomato paste

3 cups beef broth

½ cup canned diced tomatoes

¼ cup molasses

¼ cup light brown sugar

2 tablespoons yellow mustard

2 tablespoons kosher salt

These baked beans are made the way they're meant to be. They don't start out of a can, and they don't take any shortcuts on the way to becoming delicious. All they get is plenty of time and layers of flavor.

**1.** In a large bowl, soak the beans in the water overnight.

**2.** The next day, drain the beans, place them in a large oven-safe pot, and cover them with fresh water by 2 inches.

**3.** Bring the water to a boil over high heat, then reduce the heat to low and simmer for 30 to 35 minutes or until the beans are tender; drain.

**4.** Preheat the oven to 350°F.

**5.** Wipe out the pot and cook the bacon over high heat for 1½ to 2 minutes, or until it is crisp on one side.

**6.** Reduce the heat to medium, flip the bacon, and cook the other side for 1 to 2 minutes.

**7.** Remove the bacon from the pot and set it aside.

**8.** Reduce the heat to low, add the tomato paste to the pot, and cook for 1 minute.

**9.** Add the beans, beef broth, tomatoes, molasses, sugar, mustard, and salt.

**10.** Crumble in the bacon, transfer the pot to the oven, and bake for 70 to 80 minutes, or until thickened.

# FANCY MAC 'N' CHEESE

**SERVES 8**

PREP TIME: 10 MINUTES

COOK TIME: 35 MINUTES

1 teaspoon kosher salt, plus more for the boiling water

2½ cups dried macaroni

¼ cup unsalted butter

5 tablespoons all-purpose flour

3 cups milk, warmed

1 tablespoon salt

Pinch cayenne pepper

1 teaspoon freshly ground white pepper

¾ pound Gruyère cheese, grated

1 cup seasoned breadcrumbs

There's good mac and cheese, and then there's this mac and cheese. Sure, it might seem like a lot of steps just for some cheesy pasta, but when you're paying tribute to the greats, you've got to do it right. The ingredients matter just as much as the technique, of course, which is why this recipe doesn't skimp on the cheese: Gruyère, please.

1. Preheat the oven to 350°F.

2. Fill a large pot with water and salt it until it tastes like the sea.

3. Add the macaroni to the pot. Cook for 5 minutes, or until al dente, and drain.

4. Meanwhile, in a large, oven-safe skillet, melt the butter over medium heat until the foam subsides.

5. Add the flour and whisk continuously for 3 to 5 minutes, or until the mixture is smooth and light brown.

6. Add the milk and bring to a boil. Watch to make sure it does not boil over.

7. When it comes to a boil, reduce the heat to a simmer and whisk continuously until the sauce coats the back of a spoon.

8. Season with the salt, the cayenne pepper, and the white pepper, and stir in the macaroni and cheese.

9. Top with the breadcrumbs, and transfer the skillet to the oven. Bake for 15 to 20 minutes, or until the top browns.

10. Divide the macaroni and cheese among 8 plates and serve immediately.

# MEASUREMENT CONVERSIONS

### VOLUME EQUIVALENTS (LIQUID)

| US STANDARD | US STANDARD (OUNCES) | METRIC (APPROXIMATE) |
|---|---|---|
| 2 tablespoons | 1 fl. oz. | 30 mL |
| ¼ cup | 2 fl. oz. | 60 mL |
| ½ cup | 4 fl. oz. | 120 mL |
| 1 cup | 8 fl. oz. | 240 mL |
| 1½ cups | 12 fl. oz. | 355 mL |
| 2 cups or 1 pint | 16 fl. oz. | 475 mL |
| 4 cups or 1 quart | 32 fl. oz. | 1 L |
| 1 gallon | 128 fl. oz. | 4 L |

### OVEN TEMPERATURES

| FAHRENHEIT (F) | CELSIUS (C) (APPROXIMATE) |
|---|---|
| 250° | 120° |
| 300° | 150° |
| 325° | 165° |
| 350° | 180° |
| 375° | 190° |
| 400° | 200° |
| 425° | 220° |
| 450° | 230° |

### VOLUME EQUIVALENTS (DRY)

| US STANDARD | METRIC (APPROXIMATE) |
|---|---|
| ⅛ teaspoon | 0.5 mL |
| ¼ teaspoon | 1 mL |
| ½ teaspoon | 2 mL |
| ¾ teaspoon | 4 mL |
| 1 teaspoon | 5 mL |
| 1 tablespoon | 15 mL |
| ¼ cup | 59 mL |
| ⅓ cup | 79 mL |
| ½ cup | 118 mL |
| ⅔ cup | 156 mL |
| ¾ cup | 177 mL |
| 1 cup | 235 mL |
| 2 cups or 1 pint | 475 mL |
| 3 cups | 700 mL |

### WEIGHT EQUIVALENTS

| US STANDARD | METRIC (APPROXIMATE) |
|---|---|
| ½ ounce | 15 g |
| 1 ounce | 30 g |
| 2 ounces | 60 g |
| 4 ounces | 115 g |
| 8 ounces | 225 g |
| 12 ounces | 340 g |

# EQUIPMENT & SUPPLIES

## SMOKERS AND BARBECUE ACCESSORIES

**Barbecues Galore**
www.bbqgalore.com

**BBQ Pits by Klose**
www.bbqpits.com

**Big Green Egg**
www.biggreenegg.com

**Cookshack**
www.cookshack.com

**Hasty-Bake**
www.hastybake.com

**Hawgeyes BBQ**
www.hawgeyesbbq.com

**Ole Hickory Pits**
www.olehickorypits.com

**Restaurant Equippers**
www.equippers.com

**Weber**
www.weber.com

**Webstaurant Store**
www.webstaurantstore.com

## WOOD AND FUEL

**Lowe's**
www.lowes.com

**Mark's Tree Farm**
www.bestbarbecuewood.com

**Smokinlicious**
www.smokinlicious.com

**Upchurch Smoking Wood**
www.cookingfirewood.com

# RESOURCES

## MEAT, POULTRY, SEAFOOD, AND GAME

**Bell & Evans**
www.bellandevans.com

**Copper River Salmon**
www.copperriversalmon.org

**D'Artagnan**
www.dartagnan.com

**Heritage Foods USA**
www.heritagefoodsusa.com

**Louisiana Crawfish Company**
www.lacrawfish.com

**Mary's Chickens**
www.maryschickens.com

**Niman Ranch**
www.nimanranch.com

**Omaha Steaks**
www.omahasteaks.com

## BARBECUE RESOURCES

**BBQ Brethren**
www.bbqbrethren.com

**BBQ Forum**
www.bbqforum.com

**Texas BBQ Forum**
www.texasbbqforum.com

**The Smoke Ring**
www.thesmokering.com

## BEER AND WHISKEY

**Anchor Brewing**
www.anchorbrewing.com

**Blue Point Brewing Company**
www.bluepointbrewing.com

**Buffalo Trace Distillery**
www.buffalotracedistillery.com

**Bulleit Frontier Whiskey**
www.bulleit.com

**Chimay**
www.chimay.com

**Elijah Craig**
www.heavenhill.com

**Fat Tire**
www.newbelgium.com

**Goose Island Brewery**
www.gooseisland.com

**Köstritzer**
www.bitburger-international.com

**Lagunitas Brewing Company**
www.lagunitas.com

**Ommegang Brewery**
www.ommegang.com

**Paulaner**
www.paulaner.com/en

**Samuel Adams**
www.samueladams.com

**Spaten**
www.spatenbeer.com

## SPICES AND SEASONINGS

**Frank's RedHot**
www.franksredhot.com

**Kalustyan's**
www.kalustyans.com

**Morton & Bassett**
www.mortonbassett.com

**Old Bay**
www.oldbay.com

**Tabasco**
www.tabasco.com

# RECIPE INDEX

# INDEX

**WILL BUDIAMAN** is a New York City-based food writer and recipe developer, and the author of *Handcrafted Bitters*. He is a graduate of the International Culinary Center and is a recipe tester for the R&D kitchen at Maple. Previously, he served as a web producer for *Bon Appétit* and *Epicurious*, and as an editor at *The Daily Meal*, where he ran the test kitchen. For more information visit willbudiaman.com.

CPSIA information can be obtained
at www.ICGtesting.com
Printed in the USA
BVHW02s1754211117
500908BV00004B/4/P